Table for Two

Refreshing moments for your Journey

God Bless You.
Ruby
Heather Comber

By
Heather Comber

Table
for
Two

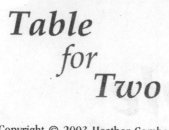

First published in 2003 by:
PowerWalk Ministries
40 Vipond Road
Whitby, Ontario, L1M 1B3, Canada
www.powerwalk.net

Published in association with Bible Publications,
Mumbai, India

ISBN: 0-9732355-0-0

A catalogue for this book is available from the
National Library of Canada

Graphics: Jonathon Hartley

Typeset & printed by:
Ebenezer Printing House, Mumbai, India

DEDICATION

*It really is wonderful to have such a large family,
and an abundance of wonderful friends. It does
however become difficult when most of them suggest
this book be dedicated to them!*

*On this journey of life, both friend and family
member become invaluable traveling companions.
For those who have walked the journey with me, I will
be forever grateful.*

*There is One who has walked, carried and stood
beside me in every kind of trial, celebrated with me in
every joy, and loved even in the unlovely moments. In
reality this journey is all about Him, and both began
and will end with Him. His strength has motivated
me, His love has carried me and His peace has kept
me. You will hopefully notice at the end of every
chapter three words will remain constant. Through
every change, through every new adventure, His love
has remained and I want to express from the bottom
of my heart that "I love you Jesus".*

This book is for You . . .

Table of Contents

Thank You

A project of this size can never be accomplished alone. I am grateful for the many friends and family who read, reread and then read once more. Also, many thanks to Rob Hayes and his staff at 'PowerWalk' for their hard work on our behalf. Rob has been a friend for many years and is now not only a great friend, but a great publisher. Thank-you!

In every life God gives special friends. I have an abundance! I have been blessed with those who continually redefine the meaning of friendship. Those who continue to surprise me with their level of love and commitment. You are my anchors and great joy on this journey we travel together.

Special thanks to Donna Ferguson who has listened to my dreams, and read my work till she practically knows it by heart! I'm sure there will be a special crown for Donna in heaven . . . you deserve it! Thanks also to Sandra Gill who for 25 years has had input in my life and has also shared my journey with this book.

Tony and Marilyn, what can I say! Thank you does not seem adequate. You are an example to the Body of Christ as you continually give of your resources for the furtherance of His kingdom.

I am blessed with parents who have loved, supported and encouraged me in my dreams. My father made sure we set our standards high! The only limitation to our dreams was to never attempt them. More than anything in life, I want to thank you mom and dad for introducing me to Jesus. I will be forever grateful that you cared enough to consistently take me to where I would grow in the knowledge of God. My mother became my taxi to a greater awareness of Him. Eternity holds your reward.

There really are no words to describe my love and pride for my children, Justin and Allyssa. They are my joy and treasure. They have already walked through many changes in life; yet continue *to amaze me with their wisdom, their love for God and their love for people. You are my dreams fulfilled! Mom loves you!!*

Into my life one day walked the man I was destined to marry. Heaven only knows what a good decision I made. My husband Murray has consistently brought new definition to the words loyalty, servant hood, and unwavering commitment. He has taught me a new level of unconditional love as he has loved and served me with every fiber of his being. I am forever grateful and thankful for your patience and understanding as together we have brought completion to this chapter of our lives. I look forward to many more . . .

Forward

During recent years the Lord has called me on a new journey. As I have travelled, I have experienced moments of loneliness. Finding myself in an unfamiliar city with an evening ahead of me sometimes seems overwhelming and quite often I will go through a fast food drive through, sit in the parking lot and endeavour to get the food past the lump in my throat. It is during those times I long to have my husband by my side, or a good friend to talk and share with. What a joy it would be to enter a restaurant and request a 'Table for Two'. A place where two hearts can meet to enjoy the wonderful gift of fellowship and friendship.

Heather and I have enjoyed this wonderful gift over the years. Our friendship actually began over twenty-five years ago when Heather arrived in our church as a new bride and was immediately thrust into the roll of 'pastor's wife'. Although just slightly older, I became her mentor.

Over the past few years, our friendship has continued to grow as we have journeyed for hours together in shared ministry, talked on the telephone, as well as planned around the committee table. Face to face we have laughed, cried, talked and prayed. I have watched Heather trust and depend on Her Saviour and encounter an intimate relationship with Him as she has spent time alone with her Lord at the 'Table for Two'.

This has been the strength of Heather's ministry and it continues to grow. Table for Two is just one more element in her desire to have a profound impact on the lives of those she has opportunity to influence. Whether by this book or by her transparent style of speaking, she inspires the hearts of those who listen. I have seen people laugh, and watched them cry as Heather shares both her journey and the intimate times with the Jesus she loves so much.

As you experience this book story by story, you too can have a glimpse of Heather's heart as I have come to know on our journey throughout the years . . .

Sandra Gill
National Director
P.A.O.C. Women's Ministries

INTRODUCTION

Table for Two

When I was a little girl I loved to read by the hour. I would find a spot where I could hide-away from the noise that accompanies a very large, busy family and let my imagination soar. Nothing captivated my attention more than the words, 'Once upon a time'. To my young mind, those words promised hours of reading pleasure where the characters of my book would come alive. Like most young girls, I loved stories that promised a happy ending. It was often difficult however to walk with the characters through the pages of their lives. Many times the suspense would overwhelm me till I could no longer resist a peek at the last chapter of the book! Although in many ways it ruined the story line, at least I could relax and live through the difficult chapters knowing there was hope in sight!

How often have we longed for the same opportunity in life . . .

I admit this journey of life often finds me wishing for a peek at the end of the book! I need to know that my 'Once upon a time' will surely have the happiest of endings . . . that my plans and ambitions were met with overwhelming success and personal contentment. However, I have learned there is One greater than I, who 'In the beginning' in the 'Once where there was no time' had already written the story of my life.

It has certainly been quite the adventure! Unlike those wonderful, predictable storybooks, I have had to learn the incredible lesson of *trust. Often on this journey through the chapters, the plot has taken an unexpected turn and I have questioned their content. I had planned to live the rest of my life securely seated in the front pew of any church where my husband was the pastor. I had written that story as a young child and was quite content to live out its pages. God had other plans. In recent times we encountered momentous changes as after more than twenty years of full time pastoral ministry my husband returned to school and life took on the unknown. During the week, his schooling took him to another city, and for the majority of time, I became a single mom. The noise and admiration of the crowd was often replaced with loneliness and solitude. Along with financial insecurity came lessons in identity, security, obedience and surrender. Murray has now finished his courses, and with the help of God, we have endeavored to begin a new chapter in our lives. There have been moments of doubt and fear, yet I have also known a divine romance that has accompanied my time alone with Him. He has seated me at a 'Table for Two' where He and I know fellowship that is unsurpassed by any other. His eternal compass has continued to be our guide, even when we cannot see what lies ahead. The journey has become not only a physical journey, but also, a journey of the heart.*

From the early memories of our childhood, to the closing chapters of our lives, life certainly is a blend of both joy and pain. It is this journey that I have endeavored to share with you. It flows from the heart of one traveler to another.

I invite you to travel with me for just a little while and find a place at your own table set for two. That place where the Lord and you will spend time together . . . that place where two hearts become one. That place where the distractions and noise of the crowd become a mere blur as you lose yourself in Him.

I have made my way to that table many times. I have laughed with Him as victory and joy have been set before me, and I have wept as in the desert land of my experience fear and uncertainty have crept into my heart. No matter the circumstances, I have always come back to the table and found Him waiting.

My desire is to bring others to its nourishment. To become a guide for those who are wandering through this journey of life. I long to take you by the hand and seat you at the table that has been spread for you. I earnestly desire that you may come to know the intimacy, the comfort and the joy that comes from spending time alone with Him. My hope is that the words of this book may be a guide on your journey.

Ultimately, this book is designed to share everyday stories from the life of an (almost) everyday person and hopefully bring you to a richer encounter with Jesus Christ, the lover of our souls.

Some of it's tales will bring you joy and laughter . . .   others may bring you tears.

My hope is that all bring you to where He patiently waits . . .

At your own Table set for Two . . .

* * * *

I LOVE JESUS

Let me seek for thee in longing
Let me long for thee in seeking
Let me find thee in love
And love thee in finding

- Anselm

I HAVE CALLED YOU BY NAME

"But now, this is what the Lord says -
he who created you, O Jacob,
he who formed you, O Israel:
Fear not, for I have redeemed you;
I have summoned you by name; you are mine."
Isaiah 43:1

My son has actually done what I never imagined he would . . . he has left home! He has gone off to college! It's not that I didn't expect him to continue his education; I just didn't think he would ever leave me! Like any good mother, I tried every trick in the book to keep him from flying from the nest. I offered to buy him a car so he could commute, I showed him the wonderful benefits of Internet courses, and as a last resort, I even offered to home-school him! In my estimation, since nearly thirty years ago I had attended the same college, I must be qualified to teach him everything he needs to know! I threw in the benefit of home cooked meals, and an extended lunch with maybe some shopping time! None of these obvious benefits however, appealed to my son. Somehow the thought of new friends, challenging professors, independence, and cafeteria food appealed to him more than my feeble offers. Justin had grown up and was ready to make a name for himself!

I remember my first glance at my brand new baby boy. From that point, my heart was forever attached to this little bundle of humanity. As is typical for most parents, we had chosen names for either a boy or a girl, however we struggled with what to name this little life that had just landed into ours. We wanted it to be a reflection of who he was, what he

1

was destined to become and carry meaning for the rest of his life. It actually took a few days, before we knew we had given birth to a . . . Justin.

As is the case with most new babies, Justin was often restless, colicky and at one time in his infancy, very ill. He would become unsettled and at times begin to cry uncontrollably. While in the hospital recovering from spinal meningitis, the nurses and hospital staff would try to comfort him, Justin however seemed to respond to only one thing . . . the sound of my voice. When I picked up that little bundle, cradled him in my arms and began to sing or speak softly into his tiny ear, his whole body would begin to relax. The familiarity of my voice soothed his troubled heart and brought comfort to my son.

No matter how many years have passed, I still know this to be true. Often, the phone will ring and on the other line will be a grown up version of a child who still needs to know the comfort and assurance that comes with the recognition of a parent's voice.

My son has grown up . . . my daughter is well on her way. I myself am well into this process called life, however, like a tiny child I still find comfort in the sound of my parents voice. I still long for their wisdom when this voyage through life becomes rocky and unsettled. There is however, another voice I long for more than any other. The familiarity of His voice above all else has the ability to right any circumstance that life may bring my way. I know I am not alone . . .

My mind wanders to another day and another time where there was obviously great value given to a name, and the sound of a voice. I find the story in the book of John. It's really not even a story; it is just one simple line. Let me share it with you . . .

There were several women who followed their Master during His brief time here on earth. I would have loved to know them, as they loved their Lord with a passion and abandon that deeply touches and challenges my heart. The scriptures tell us they followed Him right to the cross, and ultimately, the tomb. Their loss was incredible, their grief unspeakable. Their silent and steadfast watch told the story of lives that had been dramatically changed by the one they called 'Lord'.

2

There was one in particular. Mary Magdalene was her name. She was a woman who had been totally delivered, transformed, and, liberated by her Master. Her life was now His. Where He walked she would follow. I'm sure they often talked together. I'm certain she would have joined the many who sat at His feet, every word changing and challenging her heart. She would have learned to know and recognize His voice, responding when He called her name. However, He was gone. Her newfound faith had been nailed to a Roman cross and buried in a rich man's tomb. Her life now lacked meaning, her very hopes and dreams buried with the One who had placed them in her heart.

The gospel of John tells us she went to the tomb where the body of Jesus lay. However, it was with shock and grief she discovered that the body of her Lord was no longer there. She wept with sorrow, her heart responding to her loss . . . her mind desperately trying to understand what could have happened.

Thankfully she was not left to suffer long as our Lord had other plans. We find them in the Book of John, Chapter 20:10-16 . . .

"Then the disciples went back to their homes,
but Mary stood outside the tomb crying.
As she wept, she bent over to look into the tomb
and saw two angels in white, seated where Jesus' body had been,
one at the head and the other at the foot.
They asked her, "Woman why are you crying?"
"They have taken my Lord away," she said, "And I don't know
where they have put him."
At this, she turned around and saw Jesus standing there,
but she did not realize that it was Jesus.
"Woman," he said, "why are you crying? Who is it you are looking for?"
Thinking he was the gardener, she said,
"Sir, if you have carried him away,
tell me where you have put him, and I will get him."
JESUS SAID TO HER, "MARY."
She turned toward him and cried out in Aramaic,
"Rabboni!" (which means Teacher)."

He spoke her name . . . that's all it took. Instantly she knew the voice was her Master's. Turning to face her source of life Mary's world became right once again. Her fear turned to faith, her doubt to trust.

It can be the same for you . . . it has been for me. When it appears that all is gone and my hopes have been robbed He speaks my name and I instantly recognize His voice. It is the voice that knows me intimately and in the darkest hour of my loss assures me that He has risen and conquered once and for all those chains that held my heart captive. When like a tiny child, fear and restlessness overtake my spirit; I listen for the sound of my Father's voice.

I have learned to love that voice. It is different than all others. I have heard it in the quiet lonely hours of my loss. I have heard it as He rejoices with me in victory. I have heard it's gentle song in my ear when pain and fear have raised their voice above all others and I have heard its assurance when from a seeming distance I have needed the security that His voice alone can bring.

We need to follow Mary's example. When His voice calls out our name . . . we need to respond by recognizing His. It was the familiarity of His voice calling her name that Mary ultimately responded to. Day's and hours of sweet communion were rewarded as her Master once again restored His presence to her troubled soul.

The Prophet Isaiah obviously knew the value placed in a name. He also knew the incredible power and presence of HIS name. He called Him . . . **Wonderful Counselor, Mighty God, Everlasting Father and The Prince of Peace. (Isaiah 9:6)** Something happens when we begin to speak the name of 'Jesus'. That name has the power to change every circumstance, heal every wound, and bring peace to every troubled soul.

How about you?
Do you find yourself lost, confused and afraid?
Do you sit in silence grieving?
Does your heart long to hear your Father's voice once again?
Speak His name . . . and listen closely as He speaks yours.

* * * * *

FRAGRANCE

2

"Then Mary took about a pint of pure nard, an expensive
perfume;
she poured it on Jesus' feet and wiped his feet with her hair.
AND THE HOUSE WAS FILLED WITH THE FRAGRANCE
OF THE PERFUME."   *John 12:3*

There were times I wondered if my husband was actually developing some sort of allergic reaction to me! We began to notice some changes several years ago when we would be in small confined spaces together. It was terrible . . . Murray would become teary eyed, clear his throat continuously and at times begin to cough uncontrollably! I had heard of many ridiculous reasons for husband and wife parting ways, however, this would have to take the cake!

We have long since discovered the reaction was not to me, but, to the type of fragrance I happened to be wearing. I have learned to choose wisely and use sparingly! I do have a mischievous streak though. Unfortunately it often gets me in some rather uncomfortable situations . . .

The church we were pastoring in Alliston sent us annually to Jack Hayfords' Pastors School in Van Nuys California. We were sitting in service one evening when an idea came to me. Before leaving the hotel I had thrown a bottle of my favorite fragrance in my purse. It was also Murray's favorite, however, it was one that seemed to give him the worst reactions. I wondered what would happen if I dabbed just a tiny little bit on my wrists.

I know what you're thinking, and you're right . . . what a silly thing to do! The results were worse than I ever could have anticipated. Within minutes my poor husband began clearing his throat and looking at me with that knowing look in his eye. I tried to maintain an innocent look, however, it was no use. As the fragrance began to infiltrate our

5

surroundings, my husband began to react in his usual loud way. I don't know who was making more noise, the preacher, or my husband! Guilt was just beginning to overwhelm me when the course of events took a turn for the worse. Seated directly in front of me was an innocent stranger (probably married to a nice, normal woman) who began clearing his throat and coughing along with my husband!

The gentleman turned around to look at me however I could not return his gaze. Very few moments passed before this innocent stranger who had traveled from who knows where had to get up and leave the service. There I sat watching as my husband joined him, coughing, clearing their throats and sputtering their way out of the sanctuary. I really did not anticipate such a tragic ending. How was I to know there was another Murray in the crowd! And, who would have guessed he would be sitting right in front of me!

Once again through unfortunate circumstances I learned another valuable lesson . . .

This scripture in John states that the fragrance of the costly and precious oil filled the entire house. There was no one in that home that would not have been affected by this woman's presence. Her act of worship permeated her surroundings openly displaying her love and devotion for her Master. It is very difficult to hide from others who we really are. Over time our actions become obvious. Our presence in any situation or in any room has the ability to influence for very good, or, very bad.

I learned that lesson in the 'physical sense' the hard way. My selfishness cost those around me. My desire is to produce the opposite fruit in the 'spiritual realm'. My ultimate desire, and hopefully yours, would be to bring pleasure to the One we love the most, and by so doing affect the lives of those around us. To draw others in to our worship, rather than have them repelled by our attitude and presence.

I can only begin to imagine how the heart of our Lord must have responded to this woman's act. I know His heart responds with love every time one of His children worship Him in any capacity . . . every time our hearts are poured out at His feet.

This verse also speaks to me of surrender . . . surrender so great that it can only be expressed in an act of absolute love and complete abandonment. An attitude that offers even it's most valuable possession as an expression of a heart that longs for intimacy and communion with their Lord. These are perhaps the greatest acts of worship any of us can lay at His feet. Worship becomes more than what we do, but rather, who we are . . . the deepest expression of our feelings for He who is our ultimate treasure.

I love the thought of this verse. Can you imagine a life so filled with love for her Lord that it changed the very aroma of the room. Worship on her face. His countenance reflected on hers. Adoration for her Master unable to be hidden, tangibly able to be felt, sensed and touched.

How about you?
What happens when you enter a room?
Is your love for Him visible?
Do you make a difference?
Worship Him . . . and let the 'fragrance of your
love' permeate your world.

* * * * *

I Love Jesus

7

LONGING

3

"As the deer pants for streams of water,
so my soul pants for you, O God.
My soul pants for God,
for the living God.
When can I go and meet with God?"

Psalm 42:1-2

Have you ever heard a deer pant for water? I have been told it is an incredibly loud, almost ferocious sounding noise where the whole body of the deer heaves and groans in its thirst for water. Somehow in my mind I cannot imagine the gentle somewhat dignified deer making such a scene!

Now, lets stretch our imagination even further. Do you believe David; the writer of this Psalm actually heard a deer pant for water? If he did, and he obviously did, would he want to mimic this incredible sound and compare it to his thirst for the Lord?

It would appear that is exactly what David was communicating. Pride and dignity were not his foremost priority. Neither was the volume important, but rather it was the clear and visible expression of his longing for God that was being expressed. An intense longing like the thirst of one desperate in it's need for water . . .

When our son Justin, was just an infant he became very ill with spinal meningitis. As a result of this disease his fluid intake was limited to only one ounce every four hours. For a mother, that was heartbreaking. I would watch him as he began his bottle only to be disappointed when in a matter of seconds the contents were gone. His little face would register shock and a cry of disappointment and hunger would fill the room. Justin however refused to give up. He continued to suck on the bottle with the hope that somehow there would be more, his little body desperately needed relief from the pangs of hunger and thirst that surely he must have been experiencing.

My husband and I watched an interesting documentary recently on the current water crisis in the deserts of the Sahara. It is certainly not my favorite type of program, however, the more I watched the more fascinated I became.

Apparently there are some areas of this desert that only experience a rainfall every ten years. Total villages are in danger of being annihilated due to the lack of water. Recently, several local men had lost their lives while on a search for help. Disoriented from the extreme heat and lack of water they finally succumbed to the onslaught of dehydration and fatigue. There was however good news on the way. Experts were brought in and with advanced technology they located underground sources of water that had lay dormant for thousands of years. With the right tools these wells have been drilled and gushing springs of water have appeared in the desert wasteland bringing life once again to the inhabitants of that region. You watched joy and laughter appear on faces that had once only known a desperate ravishing thirst.

As I witnessed the obvious thirst on the faces of those desert inhabitants I couldn't help but compare it to what this verse is trying to communicate to us. The expression of longing on their faces was unable to be hidden. The devastation of physical drought was evident, as it had affected every facet of their lives. However, just as evident were the expressions of relief and absolute joy when their longing had been satisfied.

That's what I believe David was experiencing. There was an obvious drought in his life . . . an evident need for the life-giving source that only His presence can provide. With his whole being he cried out for His God. In the desert land of his experience he sets out on a journey to find the streams of water that would revive his weary spirit.

We all need to make the same journey. The same intensity of longing needs to direct our steps.

As the deer pants . . .
As my infant son refused to give up . . .

As the desert wanderer's searched . . .
As Israel's king longed . . . so the words of this Psalm need to
be our hearts cry.
We need to fervently pursue the streams of living water that
flow from the only One who can satisfy our incredible thirst.
Remember . . . panting may be undignified.
Longing and thirsting are necessary for life . . .
Always!

* * * *

I Love Jesus

TREASURE

4

Have you ever lost anything extremely valuable? Something so precious that it's monetary value paled in comparison to the sentiment attached to it? I have. I've lost my diamond engagement ring, not once, but twice! There are no words to describe the horrible sinking feeling that accompanies such a loss.

Let me share my stories with you . . .

We were on a hayride and as usual I was not behaving. My feeling is why sit calmly on a bale of hay when you could be throwing it at your fellow passengers. I should have been behaving however, for in my exuberance I threw a little too hard and felt my diamond ring slip from my finger.

Fortunately I was sitting beside two calm and in control gentlemen who as soon as I announced my loss took over. They instructed everyone to sit down, stop throwing hay, and **KEEP STILL**! Jeff even had a miniature flashlight in his pocket, which he immediately began to flash around the area where I had been sitting. I really didn't expect to recover my jewel, however almost instantly we gazed with wonder at a bright and shining diamond! I felt incredible relief and gratitude. Needless to say I sat down and behaved myself!

Recently, I lost my diamond again! I had been at work and did not even feel it slip from my finger. It was hours later while driving to my parents that I noticed it was gone. We immediately turned the car around and headed for home. We diligently searched every corner of the house, however the ring was not to be found. I phoned work and asked them if they could search the store, however, their efforts were also in vain.

I went to bed that night very upset. That ring meant so much to me. It wasn't the monetary value I was concerned with as we have it insured. It was the sentiment attached to it that brought its value. I'd worn it for twenty-three years. The most meaningful gift from the one I'd chosen to spend my life with.

I woke early the next morning and went into the store before it was open to the public. I looked everywhere. I pulled apart drawers and sorted through racks and tables, still I found nothing. I was becoming increasingly resigned to my loss yet something inside of me could not give up. I wanted desperately to find my lost treasure.

Earnestly asking the Lord for His help I tried one more table. I was about to give up my quest when suddenly I heard a soft clinking sound. My diligence was rewarded as before my eyes lay my diamond. My treasure restored once again.

The moment became more poignant as I focused on what God has been doing in our life in recent times. It has been a time where the giving up of position, title and material values has been part of our walk. The thought of another loss was more than I wanted to endure. I felt I could take no more and inwardly questioned how much more He was going to require of me.

I do know the answer to that question.

I believe we all do . . .

He wants it all, everything. He asks us to lay down everything that we give priority in our life. Everything we deem necessary for our security and comfort. He does this not to bring us pain or discomfort, but rather, **that we may experience the singular pleasure of Him being our All in All. Our life, our breath, our very being.**

I felt so many varying emotions during those two experiences. I also heard His voice. Over and over the words of a chorus would run through my mind. They caused me to think deeply challenging my priorities, and ultimately, my values. I finally came to the place where I knew I needed to sing those words aloud to Him. I sang them as a prayer of surrender . . .

"Lord you are more precious than silver.
Lord you are more costly than gold.
Lord you are more beautiful than diamonds
and <u>NOTHING</u> I desire
compares with you."
- L. Deshazo

The richness of His presence is indeed more precious and beautiful than anything we could ever own, achieve or desire. In my quest to find my lost treasure, I had spent many hours and shed many tears. Nothing interfered with my goal of recovering that which I had lost. The same intensity of desire needs to launch us daily into seeking the face of our eternal treasure. Our search for Him needs to become our highest priority. A priority that is rewarded with the awareness that He is near, and He will remain, always.

There was also another lesson to learn. This one from Phillip and Jeff on the hay wagon . . .

When you have experienced a loss, don't panic, 'Be Still'. When we allow confusion and bewilderment to reign in our time of loss it only heightens the problem. It drives the solution farther away until it becomes buried beneath a pile that will take much time and effort to sort through.

Loss comes to all of us. It challenges our deepest emotions and convictions, however, He shines His light in the midst of our crisis and we again sense His Presence.

We experience the ultimate treasure . . .

Him.

* * * *

I Love Jesus

BRITTANY'S STORY 5

I come from a fairly large family. We enjoy gathering together for special occasions, or any occasion for that matter. Food, fun, laughter and memories abound. We even enjoy a good theological argument or two stemming from the fact we have several ministers in our family along with an abundance of theological degrees.

All the children are so special and sweet in their own unique way. I love to spend time with them as I watch them develop their own personalities along with some traits I recognize from their parents! There is one however who holds a special place in all our hearts. We have watched her fight for her very life as she has endeavored to overcome incredibly difficult circumstances. Her name is Brittany Chapman, the youngest daughter of my sister Patti and her husband Paul. Several hours after her arrival into this world Brittany's struggles began. Tests revealed only one lung, a heart not properly positioned, and no tailbone. The years have revealed many more problems including bowel, bladder and kidney troubles.

Her first few years led from one crisis to another. It became a fight for life as she struggled to adjust to only one lung along with her other physical difficulties. Many times my sister and her husband sat in hospital rooms hoping and praying their child would last the night.

Most of Brittany's problems are undetectable to the human eye. No one could tell from looking at her that she lacks a lung or suffers internally. However, her little legs reveal her handicaps. Brittany's parents were told she would probably never walk as the lack of muscle in her legs and back would not be able to support the rest of her body. Thankfully, they were wrong. Brittany walks with braces on her legs, but, walk she does!

She recently started school full time . . . a huge adventure for a brave little girl. We were all together for the Thanksgiving celebration when Brittany's story was told . . .

No matter the age, no matter the location, we all encounter 'The Bullies'. Mean spirited, insecure people, monopolizing on the pain of others. Brittany's bullies were in the schoolyard. They were laughing at her daily. Teasing her . . . making fun of her little legs. They told her she was different and less than themselves.

As this story unfolded all of us down to the youngest were ready to march into that schoolyard and show those little monsters a thing or two. We congregated in the living room devising a strategy and planning the defense of our little girl. In my mind I pictured Brittany followed by an army of her aunts, uncles, cousins and grandparents invading the schoolyard to protect the heart of the one we loved so dearly. We were being carried away by feelings of loyalty and revenge when we stopped for a moment to ask Brittany how she handled this treatment and how it made her feel. With her sweet little voice she answered us .

"I tell them I'm different,
but God made me this way,
and He made me SPECIAL unlike anyone else."

Immediately we were disarmed, our weapons put down, our attitudes checked! I was reminded once again of David's words from the 139th Psalm.

"For you created my inmost being;
you knit me together in my mother's womb.
I praise you because I am fearfully and wonderfully made;
your works are wonderful, I know that full well.
My frame was not hidden from you when I was made in the secret place.
When I was woven together in the depths of the earth,
your eyes saw my unformed body.
All the days ordained for me were written in your book
before one of them came to be.
How precious to me are your thoughts, O God!
How vast is the sum of them!

Were I to count them, they would outnumber the grains of sand.
When I awake, I am still with you."
Psalm 139:13-18

Brittany has found comfort in the lines of this Psalm. Her words remind us that we too are of unspeakable worth to our Creator. We are incredibly valued, loved and cared for, always on His mind, never away from His thoughts.

We do have enemies however. Particularly one. The Bible calls him The Destroyer, The Liar and The Accuser of God's children. He comes to wound, rob and steal. His purpose is to make us believe we are less than others, unworthy, shameful and unpleasant to the eye.

His apparent success is thwarted as we learn to view ourselves from the eyes of our God who is The Creator, Designer, Lover and Restorer of our souls. He marches into the schoolyard of our experience and declares, "This is My Beloved Child!" He affirms to our accusers that we are His chosen children, uniquely called and created for His purposes.

This world is not yet perfect. The Book of Romans chapter eight tell us that all of creation groans in anticipation for the day when God's perfect order will be restored. You see we all have handicaps. Brittany's happen to be visible . . . most are not.

Some find themselves paralyzed by fear, rejection, and inner pain. Others are bound by crutches created to support faltering lives. The enemy would cause us to feel unworthy and ashamed. Grace declares I accept, I forgive and I heal. The Cross becomes the meeting place for all of us . . . bullies included. It is there we find our worth affirmed, our calling and future made certain, our sins forgiven, and, the strength to walk into our world with confidence and assurance.

Tough lessons to learn . . .
Hard times for one so young . . .
Brittany is learning . . . and by her life so are we!
Brittany loves Jesus.
I love Brittany.

* * * *

I Love Jesus

BROKEN VESSELS

6

"Lovely To Look At,   Lovely To Hold.
If You Break It,   Consider It Sold."

I like so many of my female counterparts love to shop! If there is a mall within ten miles I will find it! I even find pleasure in window-shopping, however, in spite of the upcoming pleasure, this particular sign always makes me nervous! It made me even more nervous when my children were small. If I had the nerve to venture into a store with such a sign, I would hold tightly to their tiny hands lest they inadvertently break some precious and valuable treasure! If the delightful looking object is broken, it becomes worthless. The value is gone. It is no longer an object of desire.

We women know this to be true! How often do we gaze with wonder at a cracked and disfigured craft or ornament! There certainly is not a line up for dented cans at our local grocery stores! We avoid them. We pass them by for objects or cans that appear perfect and unblemished.

My thoughts travel to another time where apparent limitations and brokenness became objects of value and ultimate victory. I, like so many, grew up in Sunday school hearing thrilling stories about that brave and fearless warrior Gideon. I would sit spellbound as I listened to tales of mighty battles won for his people and ultimately for his God. I remember in particular hearing about the battle against the Midianite Army . . .

Usually battles are won by sheer force of number. Simply put . . . we outnumber the 'bad guys'. According to the book of Judges, chapter seven, the Lord had other plans!   His strategy was to eliminate the army until Gideon was left to command a mere three hundred men against an army of multiple thousands! His obvious desire for Gideon was to eliminate self in order to increase Himself. *It was not a show of human power and strength that would bring the victory, but rather, divine intervention. The Hand of the Almighty extended to the frailty of man.*

Gideon was given further instructions . . . each warrior was to carry only two things into battle. A trumpet in one hand and empty jars containing lighted torches in the other. They are seemingly strange weapons to most, however, they appeared to be essential for God's army. The Battle was to commence when the trumpets were blown and a shout was heard throughout the camp. The soldiers were then instructed to take their jars and break them. Smash them into pieces! Confused by the incredible noise the enemy began to attack each other, and ultimately, God's army won the battle.

There are valuable lessons to be gleaned from this unusual story. You see, being broken always wins the Battle! It causes our reliance not to be on ourselves, but rather, on Him. It is not the volume of the number that creates power. *Rather, it is the intensity of HIS presence that is revealed in our limitation.*

I have also found great significance in the broken vessels that each warrior carried. Once broken, these vessels revealed the light inside. Hundreds of bright and shining lanterns lit the darkness of their surroundings. The battlefield became illuminated by the presence of light.

I believe that is what God desires for each one of us . . . a brokenness that ultimately reveals Him. We often view our 'cracks', brokenness and weakness as limitations and liabilities in our lives. We need to understand they become tools for our Lord to shine through! A gift to one another, and ultimately, a gift to Him.

Recently while visiting my parents, my family and I attended my home church. It had been a difficult time, a broken time. As we had arrived late we found a seat against the wall at the very back of the building. Actually, I probably would have chosen that place as my heart was dealing with its own form of brokenness and I did not want to be obvious in my emotion. As I sat contemplating our situation, the Pastor invited the congregation to join him at the communion table. It was a time that we remembered the broken body of our Lord Jesus. I was still feeling somewhat sad, somewhat broken when I noticed who was serving me communion. It was a crippled man, a man confined to his wheelchair. With a beaming face and joyful heart he passed me the cup that commemorated the broken body of my Lord. Part of me wanted to remind that man that he was broken . . . didn't he realize he was in a wheelchair. How could he appear so happy, so content. In my brokenness, I wanted to hide, even protect my heart from further emotion.

It was then I heard that very familiar whisper in my heart . . .

I realized that in my brokenness a broken vessel had served me in order to remind me of the One who was ultimately broken for all of us. Once again I knew that He values what others do not. I understood that when given to Him our brokenness could become incredible strength. It is His presence in our life that makes the difference . . . His strength that has been perfected in our pain and weakness.

With joy I accepted the cup. With joy I remembered His broken body . . . with joy I realized once again that because He was broken, I would be whole. With joy I realized that cracks become a necessary part of life. Without their presence, the light would not be revealed. They become a means for His glory to shine through a life whose only purpose is to display His Presence.

Learn to value your brokenness . . .
Understand that being broken always wins the battle. . .
Follow the example of those who have gone before us,
most importantly, the broken body of our Lord. The ultimate battle won.
It is when we are broken before Him that we become vessels of honor . . .
Vessels of immeasurable worth!

* * * *

I Love Jesus

BOUNDARIES

7

*"The Secret of Dealing Successfully with a Child
is not to be its Parent!"*

I love my son. He has grown into an incredible young man . . .
tender, gentle, compassionate and so very handsome and smart. My
husband and I decided recently that he is the smartest person we
know! More importantly, he loves Jesus with a passion and wisdom far
beyond his years.

As with most parents, our pride knows no limits!

This has not always been the case! I wondered during those first few
years what I had done wrong! He cried most of the night from the time
I brought him home till he was almost eighteen months old! His daytime
energy matched his nighttime. There was nothing he could not think of
to do!

Sunday mornings were always a challenge! Justin would love to slip
outside and throw stones at the beautiful stained glass windows of the
church where his father was the Pastor! If I was busy playing the piano
or involved in the service in any way the young people in the church
would watch him in shifts for me. He had the ability to tire out even the
most energetic teenagers! I remember one time finding him hanging with
both of his little hands to the wooden pole on the coat rack. The teens
had decided this was the only way to keep him still and in one location!
Justin actually loved it! I almost had my husband Murray build one in
the house!

Having a wayward son (even if that son was only three) and being a
Minister's Wife was not always a good combination! When he was
particularly naughty I would get 'The Look' that made me feel like the
worst mother modern civilization had ever produced. Proud mothers
loved to drop comments in my presence on how precious and well behaved their little 'Johnny' was. I was offered suggestions for books on
how to discipline your child. There was no doubt my mothering skills

were under intense scrutiny. It wasn't as if we didn't try! Our son was just himself. Full of life, curiosity, and bundles and bundles of energy!

We had a decision to make. It was either a reform school suitable for pre-schoolers, or, loving and consistent discipline with rules based on the Word of God and the principles held within its pages.

We chose the latter. I'm so glad we did. I wish everyone could know this wonderful child we are proud to call our son. Recent years found him working with children . . . energetic ones! He would go to the poorer areas of town and visit with young children who were brought into Sunday school on the bus. You often saw a 6'3" Justin patiently running down the hall chasing wayward boys that no one else could handle. Following in the footsteps of generations of clergy he leaves us to prepare for a lifetime of service in ministry. I smile when I picture future Comber's invading their dad's church!

I love to tell the following story about Justin, as it can be an incredible lesson in all of our lives . . .

We lived adjacent to a large empty field with a lovely row of trees on it. I loved having the trees nearby, as Justin loved to climb them. He would spend hours up a tree playing all kinds of imaginary games. Every so often, I would stick my head out our front door and yell . . . "Justin are you still in the trees?" I would hear his little voice reply, "Yes Mom." And for a little while . . . I actually knew where he was!

It was late winter, the ground was beginning to thaw and the field was muddy and very wet. Several men from the town were doing construction and had removed one of the trees. As a result, a huge hole was left in the middle of the field. We told our son in no uncertain terms was he to go near that hole! It was muddy, full of water, and, potentially dangerous for a small child. We also informed him it was for his own protection and safety that he needed to stay away!

Guess again.

We were both home on a Saturday afternoon when in the distance we heard the crying and the wailing. We knew that wail very well. It was our little boy. We ran to the window and watched in horror as Justin trudged his way home covered in muck from head to toe! One boot and sock were completely missing! With tears streaming down his dirty face he told us his story . . .

Of course he had gone to the hole . . . the forbidden hole. He was just having a look when all of a sudden the 'Town Bully' appeared. (I do believe this one must have had a weekend pass from Reform School!) The bully had taken Justin's boot off and thrown it into that big muddy hole! What else was he to do but jump in and begin the search for his missing footwear! Without them, there would certainly be evidence of his disobedience! Justin did manage to crawl out, but to this day we have recovered neither the missing boot nor sock. We remain grateful for our son's escape!

We found ourselves as parents with an incredible mess, but also, an incredible opportunity! After clean up time came another lesson for Justin and indeed all of us to learn . . .

You see, none of us really like rules. Even the most angelic of us are tempted at times to stretch our limits and try our boundaries. We want to see what is so bad about whatever we have been forbidden to do or touch. These tendencies have been with us from the very beginning of humanity.

We need to understand that rules are not made to ruin our fun, but rather, to protect us from danger. When our Heavenly Father speaks to His children it is because He knows what is best for them. He sees ahead. He is aware of the deep dark holes waiting to trap us . . . to rob and take our very lives. He sees our enemy lurking, waiting to trip us and push us into circumstances that will bring incredible pain. Pain that will ultimately leave stains of dirt and shame on our hearts and minds.

That's why God builds fences, gives us rules, directions and guidelines. They protect us, they shelter us, and they lead us into safe and fertile ground.

Proverbs says it so well. Let me quote the words of one far wiser than I . . .

"Listen, my son, to your father's instruction
and do not forsake your mother's teaching.
They will be a garland to grace your head
and a chain to adorn your neck."
Proverbs 1:8.
Also . . .
"My son, if you will accept my words
and store up my commands within you,
turning your ear to wisdom and
applying your heart to understanding,
and if you call out for insight
and cry aloud for understanding,
and if you look for it as for silver
and search for it as for hidden treasure,
then you will understand the fear of the Lord
and find the knowledge of God.
For the Lord gives wisdom,
and from his mouth come knowledge and understanding.
He holds victory in store for the upright,
he is a shield to those whose walk is blameless,
for he guards the course of the just
and protects the way of his faithful ones."
Proverbs 2:1-8

Unfortunately, I've seen too many broken lives. I've witnessed too many situations that could have been avoided if those concerned would have heeded the counsel and loving advice of those who cared for them . . . ultimately, the counsel of their Heavenly Father.

There are many times I have had to learn life's lessons the difficult way. I have realized the holes are really not all they are cracked up to be. They turn out to be just a dark, muddy, and very scary place.

Behind the fence on the other hand is wonderful. The grass is lush and green. The mind and heart are at peace and the company is good and pleasant restoring one's soul.

My final advice . . .
Stay away from the forbidden holes . . . walk in the paths of our God.
There is more than a boot and sock to lose!

* * * *

I Love Jesus

28

FAMILY DEVOTIONS

8

We were having company for Sunday dinner . . . a not too rare occasion for a Pastor's home. Entertaining guests in our home has actually been a wonderful experience for our family. Our children have had the opportunity of meeting so many wonderful people from all walks of life. Both the whole and the hurting have found a place at our table and it is our hope our children have seen the hand of compassion outstretched and will remember when they become old enough to extend their own hands.

This particular weekend our guest was a family life counselor who had been giving seminars at our church. These marriage and family life seminars were not always the greatest for our family! Most marriages seem to benefit from these encounters . . . somehow I always felt worse! I knew I wasn't perfect, however, after the seminars I was always a little more convinced that Murray wasn't! My expectations were often increased till my poor husband didn't stand a chance. I wondered how we would survive a weekend with a family life specialist and hoped our kids would fare better than their parents!

As the time for dinner approached I began to feel slightly intimidated. To my thinking this gentleman was sure to have a perfect home life that included regular family devotions with a perfect submissive wife who had raised quiet, obedient children! This had to be the case. How else could he tell the rest of us how we should be functioning?

When dinner was ready we all sat down and attempted to make polite conversation. Thankfully the children were behaving and were delighted to be drawn into the discussion. Not long into dinner our guest turned his attention to our four-year-old daughter Allyssa. He began the usual childish dialogue and then asked her very direct question . . . "Allyssa, what is your favorite thing to do in the whole world?"

I felt safe with that question and I felt safe with Allyssa! She was an incredibly well behaved little girl who loved nothing better than playing house with her dolls. She also loved to cuddle and have mom and dad read to her by the hour. I knew this was one test we were sure to pass!

Allyssa looked up at the gentleman and without pausing answered him very directly . . . *"My favorite thing in the whole world is having Family Devotions!"*

I was stunned. Murray's mouth fell open! Justin who was then eight years of age knew he was sunk, how do you top that one! It was almost too perfect . . . she had no idea who this guy was or what he did for a living, and Murray and I had not given her a dime to say it! Once again I was convinced our Heavenly Father has a sense of humor!

Why did I get myself so worked up?

Why is it so important to make a good impression, often at the expense of our children?

I am reminded that the very Son of God entered this world wrapped in the flesh of an infant. He asks us as parents to approach Him with the open hearts and teachable spirits that so characterize childhood. The manual He left with us gives us some much-needed advice. Listen to King Solomon's guide to parenting . . .

> *"Train a child in the way he should go,*
> *and when he is old he will not turn from it."*
> *Proverbs 22:6*

It is in coming to a correct understanding of these timely words that we can approach child rearing with hope and confidence. When we accurately interpret the words 'to train', we find that it gives us a very straightforward pattern to follow. We as parents are being instructed to invest in our children all the love, wisdom, discipline and knowledge that our children need in order to be fully conformed and committed to God. This is our God ordained responsibility both spiritually and emotionally.

30

There can be no inflexible recipe however that will turn out 'The Perfect Child'. When we read the words "in the way he should go", we need to realize that each child is wonderfully and incredibly unique. No two are exactly alike. Each small life comes into ours with their own unique personalities, gifts, dreams and aspirations. We need to train our children with this in mind. Bring out their individuality. Lead them toward that which has been invested in them by their Heavenly Father. Be attentive to their evident talent and gifting and encourage their development in them.

As parents we are terribly mistaken when we try and push our children to be something that in fact they are not. These false expectations hurt and destroy. They crush the spirit and leave children with wounded ego's and distorted views of their own person.

Child rearing is not always easy, however, the directions are there, so clear, so full of the Father's heart. When we follow His principles we can be confident that what we have placed in their heart will come forth and bear fruit. I was thrilled that even at a young age our daughter gave testimony as to what had been poured into her life. I was even more grateful that it was at the dinner table right in front of a 'Family Life Specialist'!

There is so much to learn from one small verse . . . even more to learn from one little life that comes and forever changes our own.

I remain ever grateful for the awesome responsibility given to us.

Who knows some day I may even qualify as a . . .

Family Life Specialist!

* * * *

I Love Jesus

31

COMMUNICATION BREAKDOWN 9

Have you ever been at the wrong place at the wrong time? It's happened a few times too often for me. However, there is one experience I will always remember . . .

We were on our annual family holiday taking our children to Disney World in Orlando, Florida. We were all so excited as the children had never been before. We had planned for months. Unfortunately, in our exuberance we had packed for the same amount of time!

On the second day of our journey we decided to pull over a little earlier so the kids could have a chance to relax and swim before bed. We found a nice hotel in Georgia and stopped for the night. My husband went to the desk to check in and get our room keys. As there was far too much luggage for him to carry alone, I volunteered to bring up a load. Murray took the kids and most of the luggage and went to our room. I asked him what room we were in and went to the van to collect the rest of our suitcases.

Loaded up with luggage, I proceeded up a flight of stairs as Murray had given me a room number on the second floor. I quickly found the room, opened the door and walked in. I was chatting away as I walked in, probably complaining at the weight and volume of our luggage! Never bothering to look up, I put my suitcases down and closed the door behind me. At that moment I noticed something was terribly wrong! It was quiet . . . very unlike the Comber's. Only the soft volume of a television greeted me. The stillness caused me to look up. I couldn't believe the sight that met my eyes! Instead of a lively family filling the room, lying on the bed was a perfect stranger in what I have to admit were the whitest underwear I have ever seen! The dumbstruck gentleman never opened his mouth. He only stared in wonder at what had just invaded his room and his solitude.

For once I was speechless! Questions raced across my mind. How did this happen? I was sure this was the room number Murray had given me. I wondered why this man did not lock his door. Did he not realize there were people like me in this world? And, believe it or not, foremost in my mind was how does his wife get his underwear so white!

Finally recovering myself, I apologized profusely, picked up my luggage and tore out of that room! Through this whole scene the stranger uttered not one word! Once outside the room, door firmly shut, I yelled for my husband who immediately heard me and came running!

I did find my room that night - and my own husband (recognizable by the slightly gray underclothing). I also learned a valuable lesson. When communicating we need to speak clearly, and listen closely! Communication is meant to be two ways. One speaks while the other listens. Then hopefully, we switch. Unfortunately, this is not always the case. This interactive crisis affects more than just husbands and wives. Christian believers all too often suffer from similar cases of 'Communication Breakdown' . . .

We rush forward in prayer basing our thoughts and words on assumption and ultimately presumption. We do the talking, we express our feelings, and we pray by memory or rote without taking time to listen for our Lord's reply. We wonder at His silence while we really have not given time for His answer. We live with regret over wrong decisions that could easily have been avoided if we had listened carefully.

This habit has destroyed and ruined our prayer lives. It has robbed both ourselves, and our Lord of the true communication He desires between us. Prayer is about intimacy and conversation…a natural flow that is formed through years of talking with and listening to the voice of our Beloved.

My husband phones me regularly and I him. We don't identify ourselves anymore. We have no need to as we know and recognize each other's voice. It can and should be that way with our Lord. His voice can be heard when we listen with a heart, soul and mind totally focused on Him.

His Word tells us . . .

"My sheep listen to my voice;
I know them, and they follow me."
John 10:27

Talk to Him . . . speak clearly, and remember to listen carefully! He would not ask us to listen if His voice was unable to be heard. New levels of intimacy are the reward for the heart that earnestly seeks to know and recognize the voice of their God. Communication becomes a joy . . . time spent with Him a delight. That quiet place apart from the noise of the crowd and the distractions of the day becomes our anchor . . . a place we eagerly run to.

Make the right choice . . .

Choose to listen . . .
In communicating you will end up in the right place . . .
Together.

* * * *

I Love Jesus

TRUTH

10

I'm sure my husband wont mind me telling you. It's become fairly public knowledge . . . especially to those who have traveled with us or spent an evening remotely close to our room. The truth is, like many middle aged men, he has acquired the gift of snoring!

This horrible disease causes no end of heartache for the poor families subjected to it's devastation. There really should be a support group. . . something for the victims of volume abuse! I did find some measure of relief when I discovered earplugs. They probably saved our marriage! I have found however, earplugs are not always what they are cracked up to be. Let me tell you our story . . .

I woke up one Sunday morning. Murray, as usual had gone to the church early to make sure everything was ready for the morning service. I pulled out one earplug and went for the next however it would not budge. The more I tried to remove it, the farther into the ear canal it went. I couldn't believe what was happening however there was nothing I could do and no time left. I had already wasted much precious time and I needed to get the kids and I off to church. I found this situation very annoying, however as a good Pastor's wife I needed more than an earplug to keep me home on a Sunday!

Unable to hear anything from my right ear I tried to smile and act as normal as possible (a difficult challenge at the best of times). I think I managed fine until worship time. I joined with the congregation as they sang and worshiped the Lord. My handicap was temporarily forgotten as I lost myself in Him. However, the moment didn't last long as my son kept poking me! I ignored him. None of us appreciate being poked when we are trying to be spiritual. The poking continued however till somewhat annoyed I asked him what the problem was. **"Mom"** he replied . . . **" You are singing way too loud . . . and out of tune!"**

I was mortified! How was I to know . . . my perspective was more than a little off considering the intrusion in my ear. I shut right up and decided I'd better get this situation looked after as soon as possible!

The word soon traveled. I was bombarded with innumerable cures. Friends came over with tweezers. People poured oil and all manner of liquid into my ear trying to remove it however, nothing worked. I went to bed that night with an earplug still tightly jammed in my ear.

Bright and early the next morning I made an appointment with our Family Physician. It was another disappointment as she too was baffled and could not remove the now totally jammed earplug. She felt I needed the help of one used to dealing with such problems! An appointment was made for Tuesday evening with an Ear Specialist. I was becoming depressed . . . how difficult could it be to remove an earplug?

When Tuesday morning came, I'd had enough! I decided to forget the evening's appointment with the Specialist and go over to the Emergency department at the Hospital with the hope that somebody could get this thing out! My name was finally called and I was led into an examining room to wait for the Doctor on call.

I could not believe what walked in my room. You've seen the type before, rough, tough, former army doctor looking as if he would like nothing better than to take my whole ear off! He examined my ear and with a twinkle in his eye told me to wait while he went and found the 'Alligator Claws'. Apparently the only thing he felt would remove the earplug! "Oh by the way", he commented as he walked away . . . "It's going to hurt".

I sat for a few minutes considering my options. My decision was an easy one. I got up, peeked around the corner, made sure the coast was clear and ran for my life. I came home with an earplug still firmly in place and a husband who in my opinion seemed to be thoroughly enjoying my dilemma! I was not impressed by his apparent amusement; after all, if he didn't snore so loud I wouldn't have been in this mess!

Later that evening I went for my scheduled appointment with the Specialist whose office happened to be in a wing of the hospital. I sat down in the hall outside his office and read a magazine while waiting. I couldn't believe what happened next. Down the hall came 'The Alligator Man'. The emergency room doctor I had escaped from. I covered my face with the magazine however, it was too late, he had seen me. Looking delighted at my misery, he spoke only three words . . . "You came back" and walked away with that same twinkle in his eye.

What an experience. What a terrible time, and all over a ridiculous piece of silicone! After the Specialist stopped laughing it took only a matter of seconds and the wretched thing was out. Freedom at last!

Once again I was reminded of the spiritual application. There are lessons to be learned from every part of life. The good, the bad, and even the ridiculous, which seem to happen all too often to me!

When we take a close look at the scriptures we see that Jesus often addressed the issue of our ability to hear and paralleled it to our relationship with Him. In fact He is often quoted as saying, **"Let he that has ears to hear, let him hear"**. There is a great deal of difference between hearing, and listening with a heart that desires to understand what is being communicated. So often in life we cannot hear clearly because of pre-conceived ideas and negative attitudes that have found a home in our hearts and our minds. We allow blockages to intrude into our thinking that cause the message to be blurred, or lost entirely.

When words of correction or reproof are spoken, we tune out the speaker by sticking our spiritual finger in our ear and refusing to listen to the voice we know is calling us to truth. Once confronted with truth we run, unable to take the pain confrontation will bring. We decide it far easier to live with the problem than to deal with it. We are left with uncomfortable intrusions that stay hidden and undetected by the human eye.

I see it in our lives. I even see it in our churches. It causes us as people to lose balance, sing off key, and send out a noise that is unpleasant to those around us. It cripples our churches as we sweep things under the carpet and choose to ignore integrity and truth. In trying to handle things our way, find the easy route, the quick fix; we miss the One who alone can help . . . **'The Specialist'**.

Truth is not always pleasant. Circumstances are not always easy to face, however, I am reminded of the words of our Lord as written in the Gospel of John chapter 8:32 . . . **"Then you will <u>know</u> the truth, and the truth will set you free."**

It is in the 'knowing' we are free. It is in facing the truth we can bring change and correction. For the Ear Specialist it took only moments for his work to be accomplished. The fear of the pain had certainly super-seded reality. When we open our hearts and minds to the work of the Great Physician He can very gently accomplish what looks to be too painful and difficult to face.

We all need to stop our running.

We need to cast aside our fear and remove those obstacles . . . lift up the carpet and sweep out the lies that cause our path to be unsteady.

Our reward will be a life that walks in truth . . .

A life that knows freedom!

* * * *

I Love Jesus

PITIFUL

11

"Wounds from a friend can be trusted."
Proverbs 27:6

A s is the case with most mother's I find myself increasingly proud of my daughter. Her sweet and sensitive nature makes her lovely in every way.

Allyssa was my vindication from heaven! Living proof I could handle this whole concept of 'mothering'. She came into this world with a smile on her face and was born to please. When she was younger the people in our congregation would line up to get a hug or just a 'hello' from our little girl! They would do anything for her. This was evident one Sunday morning when I found one of our staunch, serious minded elders dancing around the foyer with Allyssa in hand. She had grabbed both his hands in hers and said "Dance with me please" ...and dance he did!

She did have a problem however that can be identified with many three and four year old children. In her efforts to sound grown up and sophisticated she would often get her words mixed up.

My husband with his mislead sense of humor decided to monopolize on this habit of Allyssa's. She had asked him in her childlike innocence what the meaning of 'pitiful' was. Instead of giving the appropriate answer he taught our trusting three year old that it was a wonderful thing to say to people and it meant they were very beautiful! As a result our little angel circulated throughout the church telling everybody and anybody she saw they were very, very pitiful.

People at first did not know how to respond. Thankfully the word soon got around that it was the work of her father and not the unkind words of this child they adored! It soon became the sought after compliment. People eagerly anticipated Allyssa's words every week!

'Pitiful' . . . not a nice word normally, however, from 3 year old Allyssa it was adorable. It reminded me that even the harshest words sound

41

beautiful when coming from a pure heart . . . one motivated by love.

I have found in life we sometimes need to hear things that are not always pleasant to our ears. The spoken truth can hurt however it can also benefit greatly when spoken by a loving and faithful friend.

I have experienced this in my own life and remain ever grateful for the counsel of a friend. I remember a time I was running off course and ignoring the prompting of the Spirit. It took the words of my dear friend Lori to bring my life back in line. They were not pleasant endearing words, but rather words of correction and strong counsel. I fear what might have happened if I had chosen to ignore the words of one who loved me unconditionally and desired the best for my life.

Not all stories end so happily, not all mean so well. Some words are not beneficial. The words of betrayal, hidden agendas, and jealousy are never, ever precious. They hurt, wound, and destroy. They cut deeply and hurt intensely often leaving pain and disillusionment to those scared by them.

The scripture says . . . **"A word aptly spoken is like apples of gold in settings of silver"** (Proverbs 25:11). They give us the best of both worlds. The richness of love and friendship, along with the incredible value of correction and reproof.

How about you . . . what words flow from your lips?

Do you understand the power of the tongue?

Do you realize our words have the power to bring life or defeat to any given situation?

Choose your words wisely.

Make them your gift . . . a treasure passed from one heart to another wrapped in the lining of one whose only motivation is the well being of the other.

Pitiful or beautiful . . .

The choice is yours!

* * * *

I Love Jesus

PERSPECTIVE 12

H ave you ever heard a story that is so funny you feel obligated to share it! I have one absolutely hilarious Christmas story I love to tell. In fact, I often use it as an icebreaker to get everybody relaxed before I speak. I remember one occasion where one poor lady laughed for the entire service!

I've decided to tell you this story with the hope that you find it as funny as I did . . .

My mother was at a session with her Chiropractor when the tale was first told. Another client of his had unloaded her misery while getting her bones back in shape . . .

It had been a beautiful sunny day, perfect for doing some much needed Christmas shopping. The subject of our story had decided to do some groceries before her major shopping and rather than cart her food around she put her grocery bags in the car. She placed them in the back window leaving the trunk empty for other purchases.

Hours later with her shopping completed, she returned to her car, put her purchases in, buckled up, and prepared to leave the parking lot. Almost immediately she heard an incredibly loud bang followed by a painful sensation on the back of her neck. Her first thought was "Help me Lord . . . I've been shot!"

Panic took over common sense. Thankfully like most modern women she happened to have a cell phone handy! Shaking with fear, death at her doorstep, she called 911. The operator quickly responded asking the poor woman what her trouble was. "A drive-by shooting", she replied. "I've been hit on the back of my neck and I am unable to move". The operator tried to calm the woman down in order to get the necessary information from her. Finding her location, she instructed the woman not to panic. Police and Ambulance would be there in a matter of moments.

The poor woman, scared half to death, somehow found the courage to put her hand behind her head to see what she could feel. It was a horrible, gooey mess. Inwardly she hoped she would survive until the ambulance arrived.

True to their word, the Police arrived within minutes. They quickly found the car that matched the description and found the terrified woman inside. What greeted them however was not the disaster they had feared it to be . . .

Unable to disguise the smirks on their face they instructed the frightened woman to unlock the door. What happened next was either the greatest relief she had ever experienced or the most embarrassing moment of her life. Plastered all over the back of the woman's neck was not flesh and blood, but rather, Pillsbury biscuit dough! After being left in the hot sun, the frozen container had expanded and literally exploded hitting the woman right in the back of the neck.

Can you believe it . . . this really happened!

What a relief it must have been . . . it was not the dreaded Angel of Death . . . it was The Pillsbury Dough Boy!

What is it about human nature . . . why do we always imagine the worst? We can create a disaster out of almost any situation. However, there are definitely the special cases! You know the type 'The Doomsdayers'. Most of us have met them. A few poor souls may even have to live with them! One small cloud is sure to become a hurricane with certain disaster on the horizon. One sniffle will ultimately lead to pneumonia and hi-cups are an indication of oncoming ulcers. These poor souls live in constant fear of war and calamity, their world hangs by a mere thread.

The fact of the matter is there is trouble all around us. We don't have to look far to be confronted with negative circumstances. Job, a man who definitely knew hardship and difficulty expresses it so adequately

... **"Man born of woman is of few days and FULL OF TROUBLE."** (Job 14:1). This attitude seems to be timeless, with us from the beginning.

There is however an answer to our constant misgivings. Believe it or not my husband found it in one of his favorite movies, the Disney classic 'Pollyanna'. He actually has been known to recommend this movie during his counseling sessions. Pollyanna played a game called 'The Glad Game'. It drove the resident 'Doomsdayer' crazy as the object of the game was to seek out and find good in every situation no matter how negative the circumstances appeared to be.

It may become a game we should all engage in for there is good to be found in every situation if we choose to look for it. There are hero's all around us ... people living, loving, and making a difference for the better in their world.

For the Believer there is even better news found in Paul's letter to the church in Rome ...

"And we know <u>that in all things</u> God works for the good of those who love him, who have been called according to His purpose."

Romans 8:28

Good can be found ... it's never too far away. In each and every situation a loving and sovereign God is working for our ultimate good! What appears to be our undoing is often the road that leads us on to a richer, fuller life. What feels to be an intrusion, indeed what seems to come from behind and hit us in the head is often the catalyst to new heights on this journey of life!

Be encouraged in those times of seeming defeat and loss ...
Look for the hidden treasures that sometimes lie beneath the
shroud of darkness ...
Rejoice and be glad in the goodness of our God ...
And oh, by the way ...
Be careful what you leave in the sun!

* * * *

I Love Jesus

DIVINE INTERRUPTION

13

"I remember my affliction and my wandering, the bitterness and the gall.
I well remember them, and my soul is downcast within me.
Yet this I call to mind and therefore I have hope:
Because of the Lord's great love we are not consumed,
for his compassions NEVER fail.
They are new every morning; great is your faithfulness.
I say to myself, "The lord is my portion; therefore I will wait for Him."
The Lord is good to those whose hope is in Him,
it is good to wait quietly for the salvation of the Lord.
Let him sit alone in silence, for the Lord has laid it on him.
Let him bury his face in the dust - there may yet be hope.
Let him offer his cheek to one who would strike him, and let him be filled with
disgrace.

For men are not cast off by the Lord forever.
Though he brings grief, he will show compassion, so great is his unfailing love.
For he does not willingly bring affliction or grief to the children of men.

Who can speak and have it happen if the Lord has not decreed it?
Is it not from the mouth of the Most High that both calamities and good come?
I called on your name, O Lord, from the depths of the pit.
You heard my plea: "Do not close your ears to my cry for relief."
You came near when I called you, and you said, "DO NOT FEAR."
O Lord you took up my case; you REDEEMED my life."
Lamentations 3:19-33 37-38 & 55-58

The major theme of the book of Lamentations is the Prophet Jeremiah's complaint to the Lord. I ask you what good can come out of a book of complaining?

Life was tough for a prophet such as Jeremiah; however, he had a message of restoration and reconciliation to deliver from the heart of his God. God's people had wandered from the safety of the Father's ways and He wanted them back. Unfortunately, human nature being as it is, Jeremiah's message was not received. In fact, he was despised for his words. Like Joseph before him, his brethren silenced his voice by throwing him into a dark lonely pit.

I can't imagine what it must have felt like. I certainly would not adapt well to my new environment! This unwanted prophet found himself surrounded by dark, muddy and silent walls. He must have experienced the intense emotions of rejection, loneliness, and anger, and of course, there were always the many questions. Where are you God? I only did what you asked me to do. Is this the reward for faithfulness and obedience?

There was obviously another power at work for in the middle of all this sorrow and affliction comes what I have learned to call the 'Divine Interruption'. Perspective is perhaps a better word as we see Jeremiah bring his life once again into the eternal focus. The opening verses of this chapter show us that Jeremiah definitely remembered his affliction, yet, he remembered his God. His steadfast, compassionate, faithful God . . . the God who was His portion, and ours.

Jeremiah speaks out through the ages. His voice now echoes off those dark muddy walls. His message brings peace. His words soothe and comfort. He reminds us that even in the pit of despair our God will be faithful. A new morning will dawn and we will rise with it.

The words of this chapter cause us to remember that no matter how dark and impossible our situation may appear, it too will pass. We are not cast aside forever; instead, we are forever loved.

Jeremiah reminds us of our own life.
We groan . . . we weep . . . we lament our troubles.
He interrupts . . .
And
We remember.

* * * *

I Love Jesus

THE POTTER

14

This is the Word that came to Jeremiah from the Lord:
"Go down to the potter's house, and there I will give you this message."
So I went to the potter's house, and I saw him working at the wheel.
But the pot he was shaping from the clay was marred in his hands;
so the potter formed it into another pot, shaping it as seemed best to him.
Then the word of the Lord came to me:
"O house of Israel, can I not do with you as this potter does?" declares the
Lord.
"Like clay in the hand of the potter,
so are you in my hand, O house of Israel."
Jeremiah 18:1-6

What amazing truths we find in this picture Jeremiah paints for us . . .

I visualize an ancient potter, work-worn hands busy at the wheel. He sits on a stool surrounded by all manner of broken jars, pots and lumps of clay. On the shelf for all to see are his finished creations. Beautiful beyond description . . . without flaw . . . evidence of time, love and the tender touch of the potter. His face is kind and gentle, yet exudes power and an unwavering strength. It's his eyes however that hold my gaze. I find myself lost in them. I become one with Him, a part of his on-going creation. In these eyes I find the acceptance I seek. The knowledge that I too am in His hands, a vessel being made ready for use. The Potter lifts me from the demands and expectations of the world around me and shows me complete affirmation and acceptance regardless of how I may appear to others.

I hate to leave the potter's shop for outside it's safe walls often lie another cold reality. In this world of ours there is the temptation to grow impatient with our work, to throw away that which appears unsuccessful, and, to hide from public eye that which is not pleasing to look upon. We find our self-worth diminishing as we are measured by standards impossible to attain.

My friend Lori who I'm sure will forgive me for telling this story, provides us with a perfect illustration. Lori is a fabulous cook. Her meals are wonderful, it's just her baking that needs a little help. We had three functions at our church over the course of a week. As is typical of church functions we were required to bring food. Lori decided to bake banana bread, which was a big mistake! At the first function her bread was placed with the other deserts on the table. Nobody touched it. Even I as her friend passed it by. The second function came and with it came Lori's banana bread. Again Lori wrapped it up and brought it home. Undaunted by this obvious rejection her banana bread appeared once more only to be taken home again. We were visiting at her home a few days later when the infamous banana bread made it's final curtain call. I couldn't believe her persistence. In spite of the ongoing rejection she really believed somebody would actually eat and enjoy the fruit of her labor. To be honest, in spite of the fact that it was nearly a week old, it really wasn't that bad!

Lori's persistence amazed me. I would have given up at the very first sign of rejection. Not Lori. She made it. She believed in it! She found pleasure in the work of her hands.

She reminded me of my Potter. He believes in me. In spite of reputation, obvious flaws and imperfections, there I remain in His hands being prepared for His use. There are times He makes me visible. He brings me out to show the world His creation. I wonder at His wisdom. I fear people will see my faults and obvious shortcomings. He remains undaunted . . . His faith in His child unwavering.

Often in life our shortcomings and weakness bring us a sense of alienation and loneliness. We feel forgotten, or even rejected when our obvious mistakes and flaws become evident to those around us. Personal failure replaces confidence and security, however, there is One whose love and dedication knows no limit. There is comfort to be found in the fact that this vessel, broken though it is at times, never leaves His hands.

There we remain safe and secure while He firmly corrects and lovingly shapes.

I have been known however to react when the squeezing and stretching come my way. A few loud groans have escaped my lips from time to time. There is another valuable lesson I have learned from the Potter's shop. When the Potter is forming the clay and is satisfied with His work, he places the vessel in the oven to bake and finish. He knows His work is done when He actually hears a humming noise coming from the clay in the oven. The intense pressure of the heat produces melody in the vessel.

It can be the same for us. THE PRESSURE CAN PRODUCE PRAISE! The wise potter knows this. He allows the furnace and flames of affliction to burn away wrong attitudes, impurities, and secret sin that mar the beauty of the potters work. He knows their absence will give birth to song. Praise will flow from a heart and life that has been refined in His care.

I have often questioned what noise can be heard from me when I find myself in the oven! In spite of all my humming I'm quite sure I'm not fully baked! I will remain in His Hands. It is best for me to do that. I would encourage you to as well.

There is a song I love to sing to the One who holds every one of us in His Hands . . . my Potter.

Join with me as together we make it our prayer to Him . . .

> *"Have thine own way Lord*
> *Have thine own way*
> *You are the Potter*
> *I am the clay*
> *Mold me and make me*
> *After thy will*
> *While I am waiting*
> *Yielded and still."*
> *- Adelaide A. Pollard & George C. Stebbins*

* * * *

I Love Jesus

THE FURNACE

15

Growing up with the opportunity to attend Sunday school was a wonderful experience, which I will always be grateful for. I especially loved the adventures of God's children as recorded in the books of the Old Testament.

Sunday School did have its drawbacks though! A few technical errors were made in order to keep things simple for our young unlearned minds!

I was particularly fascinated by the story of the three young Hebrew men who were thrown into the fiery furnace. Their names were **Shadrach, Meshach,** and **Abed-Nego**. Here's where the slight error appears! Our teachers knowing our little mouths and minds would have a hard time remembering and pronouncing these difficult names offered little poems to help us . . .

How about . . . Shake the Bed, Make the Bed and Into Bed we Go! Or there is the classic . . . My shack, your shack and a bungalow!

I still find myself repeating these little rhymes to make sure I get things straight! However, it is not how we pronounce or spell their names that becomes important, but rather the lessons we remember and continue to learn from their lives. Lessons I have learned that have totally changed my perspective on God's sovereignty and our willingness to stand for righteousness at any cost.

These three young men had been carried away from home and family during the Babylonian captivity. The Babylonians had conquered all the provinces ruled by the Assyrians and had consolidated their empire into an area that covered much of the Middle East. They had a problem however. They were left with the huge job of governing a very diversified kingdom over an incredibly large expanse of land. As this would require skillful administration their solution was to find slaves who were educated and possessed the necessary skills to help govern. Because of their obvious wisdom, knowledge and handsome appearance these three young men were chosen for positions in the King's Palace.

Jealousy became an issue. Human nature remains timeless. These young men had risen to the top quickly and there were those who were not pleased! Those who had let the seeds of jealousy and hatred grow in their heart devised an evil trap for these innocent young men. Knowing the Hebrew men bowed their knee to the only true and living God they built a golden image and had the King command all to bow down and worship it. Of course the Hebrew young men refused. This did not go over well. Actually, it never does with those who are enemies of Truth.

The King was informed. Furious at their stand, he ordered them thrown into the furnace. Not a normal furnace, so great was his rage that the furnace was heated seven times hotter than usual. The jealous hearts were satisfied. Their competition . . . soon to be eliminated!

We know the rest of the story so well . . . the young men were bound by ropes and led to their certain death. The heat of the furnace was so intense that the men ordered to throw them in were immediately killed. I don't know about you but I'd take this as a divine opportunity and run for my life!

Thankfully their courage and integrity exceeds my own. They stayed to face their foe and were thrown into the onslaught of hungry flames. Those observing however looked on with awe as they noticed these young men remained untouched by the flames, not even a hair on their heads was singed. Only the ropes that had held them in bondage were completely gone.

The King was amazed and fearful. Apart from the fact that the fire was not destroying them, there was another mystery to account for. He had ordered three young men thrown into the furnace . . . he now saw four men walking around freely. The Angel of the Most High was in the flames with them.

What an amazing story! From it I have learned so much . . .

You see, those who wished me harm have also thrown me into the furnace. You have probably been thrown in a few times as well! There are those waiting to trap the Believer. Those bound by jealousy and rage. People, striving to get ahead at any and all costs. I have learned however, they can throw me into the furnace, but it is ultimately my choice **to walk out free, or remain in my bondage.** With God's help I will allow Him to burn off those things that tie me in knots and hold me captive to my enemies, ultimately, to the enemy of our souls.

I want to choose freedom. The fire will then serve to burn off my bondage . . . nothing more. The flames will purify, refine, and ultimately, liberate! We can choose to place our focus on the intensity of our difficulty, or we can choose to take our difficult places and glean from them that which will make us better people. These Hebrew young men chose the latter. They realized who was in the furnace with them. Hopefully it will be the same with us. We need to understand that in any circumstance, no matter how difficult, He will be there. He will allow the flames of our affliction to bring in us a new level of character and Christ like-ness.

I've also learned another lesson from the furnace . . . the Hebrew men could have chosen to stay in there. They had every right; they had been thrown in unjustly. These young men were suffering no apparent harm. Why not stay in awhile to prove how mean and unfair their experience was. It would be great publicity and an awesome way to gain sympathy and favor in the eyes of the people.

It comes down to one word however . . . **forgiveness.** A process that for many is even more difficult than the furnace itself. We feel justified in our anger. We fight with feelings of hurt, betrayal and injustice. We are left with a choice to make, **we choose the furnace...or...we walk out**.

Shadrach, Meshach, and Abed-Nego chose to leave the furnace behind. It was a wise decision . . . one that was made immediately by them. For others it becomes a gradual and seemingly slow process. Sadly for some, they choose to make the furnace their permanent dwelling place.

There is release in letting go and realizing the battle is not ours and never really was. Lay it all at His feet. Ask Him to stay close while the flames burn all around you. Let Him change your heart towards those who meant you harm.

How does the story end?

The young men were promoted and the name of their God was glorified.

That's what happens in the furnace....

Our bondage is gone, our freedom is restored, forgiveness is granted and there are new heights to gain!

Hot Stuff!

* * * *

I Love Jesus

THE COLLECTION

16

T his chapter may not be suitable for those with a weak stomach!
Neither would I recommend it for those who have tendencies
toward psychoanalyzing others! I say this in order to protect
myself as what I am about to confess may lead you to believe I have
very serious problems!

When I was a little girl I had a 'collection'. Like most small children I
loved to play rough and tumble games. As a result, I always had three
or four major cuts on my body. They were the visible evidence of,
playing outside; climbing trees, falling when skipping or any other ac-
tivity children love to do. These cuts would do what most wounds
do . . . heal and eventually form a scab.

I'm going to tell you what I did one day, I'll just have to live with what
you may think of me . . .

My legs and arms had more scabs than usual. I decided to pick them
off. That is not the worst part . . . I saved them! I actually put them in
an envelope that I labeled 'My Scabs'.

Can you believe I did that! Why on earth would anybody want to save
their scabs? Maybe I was proud of them. Possibly, I had gained them
through some exciting endeavor or painful stunt! I really can't remember, I only remember the envelope. I know I didn't have this collection
for very long, as my mom did not appreciate its value as I obviously did!
You see, something inside me brought value and worth to the evidence
of my wounding. I wanted to hold on to it and show it off. The evidence
of my suffering and pain was but an envelope away! I realize this was
just a silly childish stunt, however, I have seen this in the lives of so
many I have counseled and worked with. I have experienced it myself.

There is an incredible need, a compelling drive in all of us to hold onto that, which gives visible evidence to the pain, and wounding in our lives. We so often hear words and phrases such as these . . .

"I have been hurt so badly . . . you just can't understand what I have had to deal with."
"If you only knew what that person did to me you would understand why I'm so bitter and angry."
"I will never let go . . . I can't forgive."
"It's been over twenty years since I spoke to that person and I don't care if I ever see them again."

These words become our own private 'Collections'. We hoard them, storing up the evidence of wounding and pain in our lives. We wear our wounding like a badge becoming proud of our attitude, self justified in our stand.

I believe our Father's heart breaks. He wants so much more for us. He requires that we let go, throw away the evidence and walk into freedom with Him. I realize this is difficult for all of us. We fear if we let go of our hurts they will never be dealt with. As a result, we hold on tightly.

I understand as I was wounded recently. To justify my feelings I found myself writing a list. On it I recorded every question I had, every offense I felt I had taken. It was my own personal 'collection'. A grown up version of my childhood ways. It felt good at the time. I valued its contents knowing that it was available if I needed to validate my feelings. I now know it is time to throw it out. It will be difficult for with it goes the tangible evidence of my wounding. I know however this is what my Father requires of me. He has asked me to let it go. I will obey.

You see, He is ultimately in control of our life and our circumstances. He allows every bump and every bruise. He knows holding onto their evidence will only prolong our complete and full healing. He knows because He has walked where you and I have. His body took the pain and bore the scars from the actions of those who desired to hurt Him. However, He let go. **"FATHER FORGIVE THEM"** was His cry. It should be ours.

Give your pain and wounding to Jesus. Place it at the foot of the Cross, withholding nothing. You will find that your Father has a new

'Collection' for you, one that will not rot or decay. One you will be proud to display to all those you come in contact with.

Your collection will include a new song of praise to our God, a testimony of forgiveness and wholeness, a countenance that displays the beauty of His presence and a joy that comes from a heart that is free.

"Forget the former things;
do not dwell on the past.
See I am doing a new thing!
Now it springs up;
do you not perceive it?"
Isaiah 43:18-19

* * * *

I Love Jesus

THE CHASE

17

I'll never forget coming home from work a _very_ long time ago! I was only sixteen at the time and still dependent on my parents for a ride home. They were out this particular evening however and there was no one available to pick me up. Fortunately, I lived in the city and could take the bus. I really didn't like doing that, as a long walk home from the bus stop was a pretty scary thought for a young girl alone in the city at night.

I had been given my pay that evening, however, I hadn't had time to open my envelope to see how much I had earned. I decided I would wait until I got on the bus before I checked the amount. Once seated, I found my envelope and pulled it out to look at it. Right away I knew it was the wrong thing to do. There was a man seated across from me watching my every move. I knew he saw my pay and for some reason I felt very uncomfortable with the whole situation.

The bus driver stopped at my location and I got off. Unfortunately, when the man who had been watching me stood to his feet and followed me off the bus, I knew I was in trouble! To get to our home required a lengthy walk down a street that had open fields on one side. I didn't know what this man was up to, but, decided I'd better play it safe as there was not another person in sight. I crossed at the lights and headed in the opposite direction from my home. I did this because this area had homes on both sides of the street and it definitely made me feel safer. Besides, I wanted to shake off this guy just in case he had in mind what I suspected he did. As I continued to keep my eye on 'the man' I noticed him eventually walk off in the opposite direction from me and disappear on the other side of the field. I felt good about that. Now I could go home.

Still feeling slightly fearful I crossed back at the lights and started my walk. I remained cautious however and continued to watch behind me for a few moments. Everything seemed to be O.K. causing me to relax once again. That however was a big mistake for the next time I turned around I saw him in the fields running right towards me!

Have you ever tried to run when you are scared to death? It's quite an experience. You instantly gain one hundred pounds. Your legs turn to rubber! I really didn't have time however to contemplate the law of gravity as it worked in my body. I knew if I didn't move and move fast I would be in big trouble. I ran for my life and as I ran something else happened. My mouth opened wide and I started to sing as loud as I possibly could. I should have woken up the entire neighborhood! From deep inside of me came an incredible volume of praise!

I really don't know why I sang the song I did. Looking back, it wasn't even a comforting song, or for that matter, one I would sing very often. However, I realize now that the Lord was making a statement from my heart and with my lips.

I sang . . .

> *"It is no longer I that liveth...but Christ that liveth in me.*
> *It is no longer I that liveth...but Christ that liveth in me.*
> *He lives ...He lives*
> *Jesus is alive in me.*
> *It is no longer I that liveth but Christ that liveth in me."*
>
> *- Sally Ellis*

I believe my Lord was letting that man know exactly whom He was dealing with! I wasn't just a very frightened and vulnerable teenage girl on a dark lonely street. I was HIS child. The Master Creator of the Universe was there. My Shield and Protector was alive and well, and He was with me! Nearly home, I turned around once again. The man had vanished and I was safe! Scared, exhausted, sore throat, but safe!

I am reminded of the Old Testament teachings concerning the value and necessity of praise in order to drive away the enemy. A principle I was unaware of at the time, however, one that came naturally to me in my time of distress. The Israelites were so confident in the power of vocal praise that they actually sent their choir out to battle before the fighting men!

Can you imagine us doing this today?

"Excuse me please, but before I drop a bomb on you,
I'd like to sing you a little jingle."

Apparently this strategy has had prior success. Let me quote the Book of 2 Chronicles chapter 20:21-22 for you . . .

"After consulting the people, Jehoshaphat appointed men to sing to the Lord
and to praise him for the splendor of his holiness as they went out at the
head of the army, saying:
"Give thanks to the Lord, for his love endures forever."
As they began to sing and praise, the Lord SET AMBUSHES against
the men of Ammon and Moab and Mout Seir who were invading Judah,
AND THEY WERE DEFEATED."

How about your battle?

Are you being chased?

Is the enemy pursuing you with the intent to rob and destroy?

Follow the example of the warriors who have gone before us and begin to praise . . .

Praise Him for His beauty . . . a beauty that shines in the darkness and exceeds the ugliness of the enemies' plans.

Praise Him for His holiness . . . a holiness that causes the enemy to tremble at such majestic glory, holiness that causes evil to flee from His presence.

Praise Him for His mercy . . . a mercy that guides His children through the ambushes and traps of the enemy and leads them safely home.

Something incredible happens when we do this. The enemy runs unable to remain in the presence of true worship flowing from the Child of God. Something also happens in us. Our confidence returns, joy bubbles over, and perspective is once again restored.

I realize it is not easy to sing in our times of seeming loss and defeat.

We feel too heavy. Our hearts are made fragile from fear. You need to begin. It may be a simple tune at first, however soon it will become a beautiful chorus resounding from a heart and life filled with the presence of their God.

Sing your way home!

Sing His praise and watch the enemy run!

* * * *

I Love Jesus

THE BATTLE

18

"Better a patient man than a warrior,
a man who controls his temper than one who takes a city."
Prov.16: 32
"Oh Lord let my words be tender and sweet, for tomorrow
I may have to eat them!"

I made such a mess the other day! It was the mood I was in. Angry, grumpy, and looking for anyone or anything to pick a fight with!

It was very discouraging actually . . . nobody wanted to fight! Everyone else in the house had their normal wits about them. To make matters worse, the people I was really angry with had no idea how I felt. I couldn't even tell them. They think I'm sweet! Besides that, good Pastors' Wives don't go rambling off at the mouth. We hold our tongues and smile no matter what irritation comes our way!

I carried this misery for the entire day. No opportunity to vent, no opportunity to yell. I was just about at the end of my rope when an unassuming victim fell across my path. I inwardly rejoiced at this opportunity to pour out my wrath. I consoled myself with the thought that this poor creature really had no idea what it was about to face, for my victim was a fly . . . the biggest, blackest one you ever saw! With finally a chance to let off some steam I grabbed a tea towel and started swinging.

Immediately I was faced with a problem. This was one smart fly that just refused to die. Swinging with all my might I finally struck the thing and down it came. However, when I went to clean up its remains I couldn't find it! Knowing it had landed somewhere in my dishes that I keep on a wooden rack on the counter, I pulled every dish out one by one and decided I had better clean them just in case a dead squished fly had happened to fall on them.

I was beginning to wonder where the annoying creature was when all of a sudden it appeared alive and well and ready to resume tormenting me. This time I was going to get him. Swinging again I gave it a real good whack and down he came! However, now it had landed in the vicinity of a fresh container of juice I had just made! Thinking he had possibly landed in the juice, I dumped out the complete contents of the jug! This fly was definitely making me crazier!

I was beginning to wonder if this creature was possessed when out of nowhere it appeared again and began to circle around my head. If flies could talk I was sure it was saying, "NAA NA NAA NA NAA NA . . . YOU CAN'T KILL ME".

I couldn't believe myself. I was a woman on a mission, fighting with a fly! I struck again . . . it fell again. This time it landed near the cookie jar leaving me the task of once more removing and cleaning everything on the counter looking for the evidence of its remains.

You know the rest of the story . . . I lost the cookies . . . the fly lived!

Eventually I did manage to kill that pest, however, I wasted a lot of time, energy and food in the process! Later that night in my quiet time with Him I felt His gentle tugging at my heart . . .

I was still very upset and angry. Still wanting to handle things my own way. Still wishing I could lash out at those who had hurt me. Then He spoke. It was so clear. So incredibly, amazingly God!

> *"Heather…are you aware of how you handled things today?"*
> *"Did you notice in your anger, frustration and desire to lash*
> *out you created a huge mess?"*
> *"A mess that you had to spend precious time and energy cleaning up?"*
> ***" In your desire to hurt . . . you only hurt yourself."***
> *I knew He was speaking, and, I knew He was right . . .*

So often we allow our feelings to get hurt from the unkind words and actions of those around us. Anger often accompanies these feelings. In our humanity we are left with a desire for vindication. We want to get those people! We want to ease our personal pain by inflicting it on others. As a result, we speak words we should never speak. We take matters into our own hands and try to work them out in our way and our time.

It doesn't work! With flies…or people!

I learned that lesson again. I decided to keep quiet and let Him fight my battles. It was a wise decision as life has taught me that our Father does not view things as I do. He sees the whole picture . . . a picture I could have easily turned into something very ugly.

There are two wonderful verses recorded in the Old Testament. Exodus 14:13 admonishes us to **. . . "Stand firm and you will see the deliverance the Lord will bring you today".** The prophet Isaiah tells us…**"In quietness and trust is your strength"** (Isaiah 30:15).

These are timely words spanning generations of people like you and I. It is Godly wisdom protecting our hearts and thoughts. We need to heed their advice. Don't try to fight your own battles . . . you will end up making a mess! Let Him look after all that concerns you. He asks you to remember that The Battle is His. In His time and in His way He will both heal our hurting hearts and bring restoration to the Body that is His own . . . the people who bear His name.

Let me leave you with a reminder from a very wise Prophet who I'm quite sure had some battles of his own…

> *"As the heavens are higher than the earth,*
> *so are my ways higher than your ways*
> *and my thoughts than your thoughts."*
> *Isaiah 55:9*

* * * *

I Love Jesus

GUILT   19

"He is strong who conquers others . . .
He is mighty who conquers himself."

I was raised in a fairly outgoing and vivacious atmosphere, however, with my parents there was no compromising when it came to polite behavior! Perhaps this was due to the fact that we were immigrants from England, and to the British, manners maintain high priority! I have never forgotten the influence this had on my life, and yet there have been times my human nature has certainly overruled my upbringing. My citizenship on this planet has produced reactions and attitudes that certainly supersede my good British nurturing!

I have to confess that in a recent circumstance my behavior was certainly not commendable. It wasn't that I was actually rude; rather, I reacted to a difficult situation by becoming cold and indifferent in my attitude towards someone.

To be honest, I have always known that type of response does not help matters. In fact, it really was rather unusual behavior for me. Life has taught me that responding with bad behavior only increases the magnitude of the problem. I am grateful for the influence of my parents, yet, at that moment there was another Father who definitely has a vested interest in my behavior. Instantly I was reminded of the admonition to His disciples and followers . . .

"You have heard that it was said,
"eye for eye, and tooth for tooth."
But I tell you, do not resist an evil person.
If someone strikes you on the right cheek, turn to him the other also.
And if someone wants to sue you and take your tunic, let him have your
cloak as well.
If someone forces you to go one mile, go with him two miles."
Matthew 5:38-41

I have turned the other cheek many times in my life. Indeed I have felt the sting of unkind words and actions and endeavored to respond graciously. It has been a very difficult thing to do, yet, the right thing to do. I felt a different sting this time. My heart hurt. I felt terrible. Immediately I knew my behavior had been wrong . . .

Turning the other cheek is a very difficult thing to do! It is humbling to offer those who hurt us an opportunity to strike again. It requires supernatural effort to remain gracious and Christ-like while we take the blows of unkind people. I believe however, through this experience the Lord taught me another lesson. He knows that turning the other cheek is ultimately the <u>less painful position</u> to take. Striking back not only hurts others, but also hurts us, often leaving us with feelings of guilt and shame.

Guilt is a terrible thing, a consuming emotion. The heart becomes weighted down with the cumbersome feelings of shame and remorse. Christ died that we might be free of their terrible weight. Forgiven, cleansed and walking in freedom. Retaliation in any way destroys what He came to do for us, and ultimately, in us.

I learned once again to choose my pain. The sting on the cheek will pass, however, the burden of guilt on the heart will remain and grow with each situation I feed it.

I will endeavor to be kinder next time.
I will try to do it His way.
I'll offer my cheek . . .
And protect my heart.

* * * *

I Love Jesus

70

WHY

20

"I lay my why's before your cross
In worship kneeling
My mind too numb for thought
My heart beyond all feeling
And worshiping realize that I in
knowing you don't need a why."
Ruth Bell Graham

H as the question 'why' ever escaped your lips?

Have there been times a myriad of questions have left your heart and mind numb with their magnitude?

When our children were very young, the word 'why' seemed to be their favorite response to almost every direction or answer they were given. Both had extremely inquisitive, inquiring minds and constantly sought for answers to life's everyday issues. Their little minds struggled with the concepts of gravity, electricity and the more complex issues of life, however, of just as much concern, were questions regarding bedtime, snack choices and television rules! One of Justin's more interesting inquiries was why birds could fly and yet cows could not (a fact I remain grateful for).

I must confess as an adult, I am often overcome by an abundance of questions, an overwhelming sense of 'why' . . .

I find comfort in knowing I am not alone. Others before me asked 'why'. King David asked all the time . . . read the Psalms. His looming question, and I must admit mine at times, concerned the prosperity of the unrighteous, the bad guys! Why do these people seem to get ahead while the righteous suffer?

There comes a certain peace when I realize my Lord also asked. He asked His Father 'why'. It was on the cross that this question rang out from a broken wounded Savior. I have often wondered what emotions our Lord experienced. Did He feel forsaken and alone on His cross?

We find ourselves with so many questions without immediate answers. However, there remains a decision to be made. It isn't an easy one. It will require focus not on ourselves, but rather, on Him. I believe the answer lies with our decision to WORSHIP.

My mind travels across the boundaries of time and custom to another day, another place. A forlorn, rugged man stands with his only son by his side and asks the age-old question . . . why? Isaac was the 'Son of Promise'. Indeed the future of the chosen race depended on his existence. Many years before God had shown Abraham a dark night filled with stars beyond number. These stars represented the descendants that would come from this covenant between God and Abraham. Where was the promise now? Why had God deserted them? Why must he take his precious son . . . the 'promised son' and put him to death by his own hand. Surely God must be mistaken.

Questions loom in the air as the silent figure stands against the mountain. What prevails however is not the doubt, but the trust. Abraham had the answer. It had been with him since the beginning, it would not fail him now. He would take his child and follow the call of his heart . . . the call to worship.

Listen to the Genesis account . . .

> *"Early the next morning Abraham got up and saddled his donkey. He took with him two of his servants and his son Isaac. When he had cut enough wood for the burnt offering, he set out for the place God had told him about. On the third day Abraham looked up and saw the place in the distance. He said to his servants, STAY HERE WITH THE DONKEY WHILE I AND THE BOY GO OVER THERE. WE WILL WORSHIP AND THEN WE WILL COME BACK TO YOU."*
> ### *Genesis 22:3-5*

As Abraham laid His son at the foot of the mountain, we must lay at the foot of the cross every single doubt, all anger and every 'why'. It is there we must seek the One who is beyond our thoughts and our ways. It is there we must look to His face and begin to worship.

It is at the side of the hill called Golgotha we can fully understand sacrifice . . . sacrifice that is given as worship to Almighty God. It is there our searching hearts will find the answers. Our perspective and trust will be restored. Our faith will triumph as we can be assured that He **alone** holds the answers. He **alone** can right any situation. He **alone** is just and fair, and no power other than His will determine our life and our future.

For Abraham a lamb was provided . . .
His son's life was spared . . .
Worship had remained.

It can be the same for us. In the darkness of our doubt and fear we need to leave our situation, take our seemingly broken promise and begin to worship. It is at the mountain of sacrifice and trust we can see that what really matters is our relationship with Him.

I look forward to the day when we won't need to ask 'why' anymore.

There will be no reason . . . we'll be too busy.

Forever kneeling . . .

Forever worshiping . . .

Thankful for the cross.

* * * *

I Love Jesus

MURRAY'S PSALM

21

"Blessed is he who has regard for the weak;
the Lord delivers him in times of trouble.
The Lord will protect him and preserve his life;
he will bless him in the land and not surrender him to
the desire of his foes. The Lord will sustain him on his sickbed
and restore him from his bed of illness."
Psalm 41:1-3

I really do love my husband! He has so many wonderful qualities that have captivated my attention since the first time I met him. Although our growing up years lacked much in common, this only served to increase our interest in one another. I was actually quite intrigued by someone who seemed to be so opposite to me. I had grown up in a financially secure environment and enjoyed the comforts that this provides. I attended a very large growing church that provided an exciting program with an abundance of friends and activities.

Murray was raised in a Pastor's home. He had known pain at a very young age when his mom had passed away from a cerebral brain hemorrhage before his eighth birthday. His father pastored in both rural and city settings and Murray moved comfortably in both arenas. When I met him, he was probably the most energetic person I had ever met. He never seemed to be in one place for very long. Life has always been an adventure for Murray, and his love for people is evident to everyone he comes in contact with.

These qualities of energy and strength seemed to be infallible to me. Murray was seldom, if ever, sick or tired. He just kept going! This quality however was severely challenged at one point in our lives . . .

Years ago during my quiet time with the Lord He had led me to this scripture for my husband. I really did not understand why. At the time of reading, Murray was feeling fine and life was good. However, I have learned that it is not usually a good thing to know what lies ahead. Within weeks my husband was deathly ill.

The church we were pastoring at the time had purchased property and had begun to build a new church. The church was growing so quickly we immediately went from Phase One to Phase Two without a break. After two consecutive years of a building program, Murray's body was more than a little worn out. Our family doctor diagnosed him with pneumonia, pleurisy, Epstein-bar virus, fluid build up on the lungs, and ulcerative colitis. We tried to deal with his illness at home however; it very quickly got to the point where he needed to be hospitalized. My parents drove to our home, and together my dad and I took him to the hospital where he was admitted immediately. Over the next few days, his condition began to deteriorate so badly that he needed to be sent by ambulance to a larger center for more intensive care. It had been difficult enough coping with his sickness while trying to maintain a home and a church, now I was becoming increasingly worried as he was being transferred further away from us. The whole situation became very frightening.

I had visited Murray as often as I could while he was in the larger hospital and always left feeling discouraged at his seeming lack of progress. After he had been away for a week, my doctor informed me that they would be sending Murray back to the hospital in our town. I considered this to be good news and an indication of recovery. However, I was wrong.

When I went to see Murray I was devastated. He looked terrible and in much worse shape that he had been before he was transferred. I had a horrible feeling that my husband was dying. I immediately took my concerns to our doctor who very gently informed me that there was nothing he could do to help him. Due to complications from so many different illnesses, his body was not responding to the prescribed antibiotic.

Throughout this process the Lord consistently reminded me of the Psalm He had given me weeks before I knew this crisis would occur. It did bring a measure of comfort, however, I was still very frightened! Prospects of life without the one I loved loomed continuously before me. Questions filled my mind . . .

How would I raise my children alone? We had a three-year-old daughter and a seven-year-old son. Didn't they deserve to grow up with a father?

Would my children experience the same pain my husband had when he had lost his own mom at just eight years of age?

How could I possibly bear this trial, and perhaps the most consuming question was . . . where are you God?

There were also thoughts of guilt. I thought of the many times I could have been nicer, spoke kinder, loved deeper, (and spent less money). My heart and mind sought for peace as I endeavored to live through this time. Though the pain of my situation seemed to fill my heart and mind, I felt another call. It was a call to surrender. A surrender perhaps deeper than any I had ever known. I remember coming to that point. It was not easy. It never is.

Needing to be alone, I went into our washroom and turned on the shower. With the sound of the rushing water blocking the noise, I began to scream and sob out my pain. I took it to the only One who could help. King David obviously had been there before me. His cry is recorded in Psalm 18:4-6 . . .

> *"The cords of death entangled me; the torrents of destruction*
> *overwhelmed me.*
> *The cords of the grave coiled around me; the snares of death confronted me.*
> *In my distress I CALLED TO THE LORD; I cried to my God for help.*
> *From his temple he heard my voice;*
> *my cry came before him, into his ears."*

The process took awhile. However, eventually I felt the pain subside, the fear melt away. His arms circled my weary body once again. My heart was quieted, my resolution strong. I would pray and I would trust.

I called on others to join me. People from all over the country began to cry out to God on our behalf. Thankfully we experienced a miracle. Within hours of our call for prayer my husband's fever broke and the diseases began to leave his body. God began the healing process that night, and Murray has never looked back.

My faith was challenged during that time; however, these verses were continually brought to my mind. I was reminded once again of the comfort and encouragement that comes from reading The Word of God. . .

How often in life do we miss the peace and consolation that God longs to bring to His children? The Word of God needs to be our lifeline and our healing foundation. It becomes the source that drives the diseases of fear, doubt and confusion from our bodies. We need to feed regularly from it's life giving words, draw it's promises to mind when the reality of our situation looks impossible.

I had been given the promise that God would restore Murray from his sickbed!

I'm so very glad He did.
I love you Murray . . .
And. . .

* * * *

I Love Jesus

OVER BOARD

22

Bedtime Devotions were always a special time for our children and their Dad. It was a routine that started when they were very young and continues through today.

Murray wasn't always home in the evening to help put the kids to bed, but when he was, he and the children would jump into our bed and have their own little church service! The time together would usually include, singing, a full-fledged 'testimony service', prayer requests and a Bible story. (Mom put her foot down when it came to having offering and announcements!)

Quite often when our son was off to school and Murray to the office, our daughter Allyssa would recount to me the basic message of the story she had heard the evening before. One of her stories was quite enlightening. Her little three year old mind had developed an interesting twist on an age old Bible Story.

I should have realized she didn't have a complete grasp of the truths we were teaching. She often complained that Jesus moving around inside of her was the source of tummy aches, and she took great delight in the fact that both Moses and Jesus lived inside her heart! However, during one of her story-telling sessions she in her childish way taught me a lesson we all need to learn.

I gathered from the basic content of her chatter she was trying to describe the story of the Prophet Jonah running from God. When she came to the part about the storm at sea, her eyes grew wide with excitement as she described the crashing waves and the fear of the men on board. When she paused for a breath, I asked her what the men did in order to save themselves and their ship.

Listen to the doctrine according to Allyssa. . . **"Well Mommy, she**

replied . . . they threw God overboard." My first reaction was to laugh, however, I was very quickly confronted with the truth of her comment . . .

How many times have we as Christians encountered storms in our lives, and in our own way, 'thrown God overboard'! It could be a financial disaster, the loss of a loved one, physical illness, or in any difficult place we find ourselves where we turn to every resource available instead of turning to God. The world has even known of brilliant men dedicated to serving God, who, when seemingly insurmountable trials came into their lives, blamed God and walked away from the Christian Life.

Like Jonah of old . . . we run.

I was once again reminded of the Disciples on the Sea of Galilee who were also in the midst of a storm. These men however, knew the Master of the Sea, the One who calms every storm and who today says to the storms in our lives, **'Peace, be still.'**

Just as my three-year-old reminded me, we need to remind ourselves daily that God is with us in every situation life throws our way. His grace and strength are ours by simply calling out His name.

In your trial, don't throw God overboard; instead, invite Him into the boat with you!

I can't always promise lack of storms, however when He is in your boat the journey becomes smooth sailing!

There are some timely words we need to remember when we feel our life has been shipwrecked and our captain has abandoned the boat . . .

> *"Never will I leave you;*
> *never will I forsake you."*
> *(Hebrews 13:5)*

* * * *

I Love Jesus

JOB'S STORY **23**

"Though He slay me,
yet will I hope in Him. . . "
Job 13:15

It seems our generation is becoming increasingly attracted to 'Reality' T.V. Programs that feature the everyday lives of people just like ourselves, seem to have replaced fantasy and drama in their ability to be a magnet for our attention. Programs such as 'Survivor', 'The Bachelor', and 'The Amazing Race' have millions addicted to their on-going drama.

There is a story however, that through the passing of the centuries has remained timeless. It was not birthed through the vivid imagination of a Hollywood Director, but rather, through the heart of our Creator. The epic drama of the life of Job would challenge every episode I have ever witnessed or watched on the television screen . . .

As in most stories the beginning is quite captivating. Job was a man of incredible wealth and influence. In fact the beginning words of this book tells us "this man was the greatest of all the people of the east". He appeared to have it all, a large prosperous family with seven sons and three daughters, a fortune in animals and a reputation unparalleled in his day.

Job's account tells us something else about him, words I would love to have history record about me. The very first lines of this book tell us he was "blameless and upright . . . a man who feared God and shunned evil".

It sounds to me like this was a man who definitely had his life in order. He had a respectable family, good health, abundant wealth, and a heart that was obviously in right relationship with his Creator. However, that is only the beginning of Job's chronicle. The real story often lies in the middles pages of our life, somewhere in between our arrival and departure.

These chapters were extremely difficult for Job. The plot took an unwelcome and unexpected twist. It would appear that not everyone rejoiced at this good man's fortune. The righteousness of this godly man was a continual affront to his greatest enemy, an enemy we all have in common.

What followed was a result of God allowing overwhelming circumstances into the life of one whom He dearly loved and trusted. Job's dedication and loyalty to God were challenged as devastating circumstances caused him to lose everything considered of value. His children and servants were killed. His flocks were destroyed. And perhaps the greatest challenge was to his health. The Scripture tells us that he was struck with boils from the top of his head to the bottom of his feet.

Somewhere in the middle of this agony we hear these words echo from a broken and wounded man . . . "Though He slay me, yet will I hope in Him."

It is very difficult to understand how the words 'slay' and 'hope' can appear in the same sentence. One speaks of death, an end. The other speaks of life, a beginning and a future. It is even more difficult to understand how such powerful and intimate words could flow from such horrible circumstances. It has been through the process of life however that I have fully appreciated the heart of Job as recorded in this incredible verse. I believe that Job's words flowed from a heart that knew relationship and intimacy with the Almighty.

We seldom place our hope and trust in that which is unfamiliar, and unknown. When things become difficult and life produces situations beyond our control, we lose hope and we lack trust. We feel the 'slaying' but we seldom feel 'hope'. Job knew that it was only in his knowledge of the 'Author of Hope' that he could repeat these words with unshakeable confidence. He knew it was only his God who could bring life out of death, hope from despair.

God does allow grief to enter our life. He does see our losses . . . He does feel our pain. Yet, in the midst of the very darkest of circumstances the knowledge of His Presence will bring hope. The familiarity of His Word reaches into the darkness of our situation and lights the torch of hope.

At the conclusion of most episodes of 'survivor', a contestant is voted off the island. Upon their departure they are required to take their torch and blow out its flame. Literally, the light of their presence ceases to shine. Their continued influence has been eliminated . . .

Thankfully, the drama of this man's life continues to impact us many thousands of years later. His light continues to shine, reminding us that throughout the drama of everyday life . . .

There is hope.

* * * *

I Love Jesus

SUFFERING 24

"But whatever was to my profit I now consider loss for the sake of Christ.
What is more, I consider everything a loss compared
to the surpassing greatness of knowing Christ Jesus my Lord,
for whose sake I have lost all things.
I consider them rubbish, that I may gain Christ and be found in him,
not having a righteousness of my own that comes out from the law,
but, that which is through faith in Christ -
the righteousness that comes from God and is by faith.
I WANT TO KNOW CHRIST AND THE POWER OF HIS RESURRECTION
AND THE FELLOWSHIP OF SHARING IN HIS SUFFERINGS,
BECOMING LIKE HIM IN HIS DEATH . . ."
Philippians 3:7-10

The question of suffering certainly seems to be a timeless one. The pages of history record man's struggle to overcome adversity and book after book try to explain it's meaning and purpose in our life. I consider myself still very much on a journey as I endeavor to understand suffering's purpose and benefit to the Believer.

The last verse of this portion of scripture has been the theme of my life for a very long time. I hardly know of a time when I have spoken publicly that I have not used this verse in some way. I want to KNOW Christ and this desire has led me down many paths I would not have chosen for myself. The fellowship of His sufferings was something I chose not to think about simply because I did not fully understand it's meaning. It is only in sharing in His sufferings that we do understand.

This verse became more of a reality for me shortly after our first child Justin was born. Justin had reached the age where he required his four-month vaccination. He reacted like most babies . . . miserable, feverish

85

and ill. However, this lasted all night and by morning he could not lift his head. I became very frightened. Inwardly I think I knew what was wrong with my baby, however, I couldn't bring myself to speak the words.

As usual, in my crisis situation I called home. My mother quickly raced to her car and made it to our house in record time. Together with my mom, Murray and I took our baby boy to the Pediatrician's office. He was rushed from there to the hospital where we were told he would require a Spinal Tap.

Justin was very quickly diagnosed with Spinal Meningitis. The doctors told us if he lived he certainly would not be an average student. The disease could affect his ability to function intellectually.

Murray and I were both more than a little heartbroken and scared. I knew I needed help beyond my own ability to cope so Murray drove me around the corner to the church we were pastoring at the time. The office staff was like family. They were all very loving and concerned however they knew I needed time alone and left me with my Lord. Broken and frightened, I made my way to the altar of that church where I poured out my grief. I desperately needed the comfort of His presence to see me through this devastating time.

It was through His incredible grace and strength that I was once again able to surrender and sense His peace.

I told many people I felt cushioned, I knew the blows were coming; however I couldn't feel them, He was taking them for me. My husband tells me that at night in my sleep I would hold him and rock him thinking he was my baby. I would tell him everything was going to be all right, Jesus was with him.

Indeed He was. He healed my baby boy! In fact, He did more than we could have ever believed. In grade three Justin was removed from the classroom to be tested, as his teacher believed he was intellectually advanced for his age. Her calculations were correct! Justin's test results showed a grade level of achievement well beyond his years. It was incredible . . . a true miracle!

In life most of us will experience these times of testing, these seasons of suffering. It is natural to react with fear and despair; however, we need to realize our God has reason for every situation that enters our life. He has purpose in our suffering.

There is a beautiful Psalm that has both encouraged and challenged me during my times of difficulty. Let me share the richness of its truth with you . . .

"How lovely is your dwelling place, O Lord Almighty! My soul yearns, even faints, for the courts of the Lord; my heart and my flesh cry out for the living God. Even the sparrow has found a home, and the swallow a nest for herself, where she may have her young – a place near your altar, O Lord Almighty, my King and my God. Blessed are those who dwell in your house; they are ever praising you. Blessed are those whose strength is in you, who have set their hearts on pilgrimage. As they pass through the Valley of Baca (weeping), they make it a place of springs; the autumn rains also cover it with pools. They go from strength to strength."

Psalm 84:1-7

At some point in our lives, most of us will make this journey through the 'Valley of Baca', the 'Valley of Weeping'. I have learned however, that as we make our way through this dry barren land, this place of suffering, refreshing can be found . . .

Sometimes we have to dig for springs. They are very seldom on the surface. The richest and choicest delights often lay buried well below the exterior. So it is with the difficult circumstances in our lives. Surface answers rarely meet our needs. That which is easily accessible is often just as easily lost. It is that which is submerged in the depths of our life experience that will ultimately provide our strength, that which has been nurtured through years of dwelling in His courts.

In order to uncover these jewels we need to take action. The responsibility becomes our own. When we dig deep in to our souls we will uncover the rich presence of the Lord along with the resources we need for our journey. We will delight in fresh springs of living water. Pools of refreshing will be our reward. It is from there we continue our pilgrimage walking from Strength to Strength.

Remember God has purpose in this journey of suffering. It is often the catalyst in our life that conforms us to the image of God.

He is making us look like Him . . .

The face and nature of our God implanted forever on our hearts . . .

Fellowship that knows no comparison . . .

All else is indeed . . . rubbish.

* * * *

I Love Jesus

A HOPE AND A FUTURE

25

"For I know the plans I have for you," declares the Lord,
"plans to prosper you and not to harm you,
plans to give you hope and a future. . . "
Jeremiah 29:11

S o many times we as Christian Believers have our favorite verses from God's Word! This really is not a problem. In fact, it's rather normal. The problem is only created when we fail to keep the verse in the context of the whole chapter. This verse offers comfort and hope for many believers, however this entire chapter is amazing!

At the time of writing we find The Children of Israel living in captivity. Abducted and taken in battle, they found themselves far from home and longing for life, as they had known it. Freedom and familiarity had been replaced with bondage and slavery. Each new day provided the challenge of adapting to the strangeness of their surroundings. I can only imagine the emotions of the captives. If I were there, I would do everything in my power to restore those poor wanderers to their homeland!

My actions however would portray human thoughts, ways and perspective. Conversely, God's thoughts and ways are not like our own. His perspective is eternal, far beyond the scope of our limited knowledge. In fact, the beginning verses of this chapter find God instructing the captives to settle down, build houses and plant gardens in the land of their captivity. He even told them to marry and have children, to increase and not to decrease. Most importantly, He asked them to pray for the prosperity of the city to which He had called them into exile. It sounds to me like He planned to keep them there for a while!

Here's a fact I love about this story. According to history, this was one of the most creative times intellectually and artistically for the Jewish nation. We benefit today from the fruit of their bondage.

I relate to this story. I confess I have never been abducted from my homeland and rushed off to slavery in some foreign country. However, I like so many of you have had choices made for me that were not always easy to take! I have felt alone. I have felt the sting of unjust treatment. I have also felt the helplessness that accompanies the inability to correct or change my circumstances.

I have been left with a choice we all need to make. We need to believe that regardless of how circumstances may appear, God remains in control. His eyes view the entire tapestry of our life. One stitch at a time he weaves each piece together till the complete picture unfolds. It is only in trust and acceptance that we can view our captivity as a wonderful opportunity. In fact, when we settle down and accept whatever our 'captivity' may be, it can become an incredible time in our lives. Like the captives before us it can become a time of growth, strength, insight, wisdom, and new depths in Him.

Our seeming 'captivity' becomes an opportunity to increase and not to fade away. Our prayer life becomes richer as we learn to pray blessing into even the darkest of circumstances. Hopefully the heritage we leave from these seasons will bless generations to come . . .

How about you?

Do you feel captive . . . far and away from all that is familiar and dear to your heart?

Has life taken you down roads you have never traveled before . . . roads you would not have chosen for yourself?

He chose them for you . . .

He wants to bless you there . . .

His Word is <u>always</u> faithful.

Trust Him and listen to His voice as He gently affirms those words to your heart . . .

"For I know the plans I have for YOU declares the Lord". . .

* * * *

ALONE WITH GOD

26

" When they looked up, they saw no one except Jesus."
Matthew 17:8

I am definitely a people person. I love being with people or just watching as they pass by. I find enjoyment in long chats on the phone with a good friend or hours of fellowship in one another's home. There we share secrets and funny stories, holding our sides as we burst with laughter, or holding each other as we cry. Most of all we experience life, together.

This is a good thing. God has given us one another. He created His children to be people of intimacy finding satisfaction and contentment in relationship. To know and to love one another reflects His bond with creation. I have found however, there are times when no other, no matter how deep the friendship or love, can fill the incredible need and intense longing of the soul.

There are definitely times in this journey, that aloneness becomes our experience. Often the need for others pales in comparison to the desire we have to be with Him alone in the quietness and have Him speak the words we know only He can. It is often in the darkness and stillness of the night, when the pain of our circumstances soaks our pillow with tears that we find the comfort of His presence.

I've always loved the Psalms. I'm actually very excited about meeting King David in heaven! I've planned some long talks for us, as he expresses so perfectly what I often cannot. I know He felt life deeply. I also know He knew his God. In spite of being heralded a King and leader of men, David realized that there was only ONE who could completely consume him, only ONE who could bring peace to the broken areas of his life.

Listen to the cry of his heart . . .

"Find rest, O my soul, in God alone;
my hope comes from him.
He alone is my rock and my salvation;
he is my fortress, I will not be
shaken."
Psalm 62:5-6

Into each life, times of aloneness will come. Nights of soaking your pillow will come. The beauty of theses times lies in the fact that He comes also. While all around others are sleeping He steadfastly remains. He waits, watches and listens bringing hope and comfort to the heart that has been crushed.

These alone times can become a good thing, a necessary experience.

You need to lift up your eyes till you only see Jesus.

He will be there.

He promised.

* * * *

I Love Jesus

TRUST

27

Almost every spring our robins come back. They build their nest just outside our kitchen window, which is perfect for me. I love to watch as the mother busily prepares her nest gathering bits and pieces till the home is complete. Once the security of the nest is finished she ceases from her labor to sit and wait for the birth of her young. Before long a beautiful blue colored egg appears and the countdown begins!

I find the whole process fascinating to watch. There is one aspect however that challenges me as I watch it unfold every year. It's the small, helpless and so very vulnerable baby robins. Totally dependant on their mother for their every need, these helpless young are often left alone in the nest while she flies off to find food. When the sought after nourishment is found, the mother flies home to drop it into the open beaks of her waiting babies.

What I find incredible is that the beaks of the baby robins remain wide open and ready, waiting for the return of the mother even while she is absent from the nest. From my perspective I don't believe these baby robins have their sight. Their tiny eyes remain shut while their mouths remain open, waiting in total trust and eager anticipation. It would not appear they experience a moment of doubt. They seem certain that the necessities of their existence are but a flight away.

As I watch this scene every spring I feel the same gentle nudge in my spirit. He speaks once again . . .

"Heather do you trust Me?"
"Are your heart and mind open continuously ready to be fed?"
"Do you expect my presence?"
"Do you long for me with hunger and eagerness?"
"When seasons of life darken your awareness of Me will you continue to trust that I will provide though I seem far away?"

These are tough questions ultimately challenging our level of trust and our ability to wait in the darkness. We too are helpless and vulnerable. We need Him for everything . . . our life, our breath and our very being. When circumstances arise that leave us unable to provide for ourselves we feel alone and abandoned in our nest. Fear demands a place in our heart, as we cannot see His hand on the horizon.

I find a certain peace when I watch the mother robin return to her young, I am reminded once again that my provider, my loving parent, my faithful Father will come. He always does for He cannot fail. In His hand He brings all I need to sustain and keep me for another day.

Once again I find the longings of my heart recorded in the words of Israel's king. David wrote these words in the desert's of Judah. I seriously doubt there were robin's building their nest in this dry barren land, however, there is evidence of a longing heart . . . a searching soul waiting for the coming of his God.

Listen to David's cry . . .

"God, you are my God, earnestly I seek you;
my soul thirsts for you, my body longs for you,
in a dry and weary land where there is no water.
I have seen you in the sanctuary and beheld your power and your glory.
Because your love is better than life, my lips will glorify you.
I will praise you as long as I live, and in your name I will lift up my hands.
My soul will be satisfied, as with the richest of foods;
with singing lips my mouth will praise you.
On my bed I remember you; I think of you through the watches of the night.
Because you are my help, I sing in the shadow of your wings."
Psalm 63:1-7

Like those tiny robins . . .

Like the cry of hunger from the desert . . .

We need to wait . . .

We need to anticipate . . .

We need to eagerly expect His coming.

Feed us Lord.

* * * *

PROVISION

28

"Though the fig tree does not bud
and there are no grapes on the vines,
though the olive crop fails
and the fields produce no food,
though there are no sheep in the pen
and no cattle in the stalls,
yet I will rejoice in the Lord,
I will be joyful in God my Saviour.
The Sovereign Lord IS my strength;
he makes my feet like the feet of a deer,
He enables me to go on the heights."
Habakkuk 3:17-18

I have always loved these verses . . . I remember a time in recent
years when the reality of these verses were very much part of our
life. Habakkuk and I were definitely experiencing the same emotions! I can remember it being the month of September with our pay
check about to run out in mid November. I wanted to prepare ahead,
store up for our certain time of need. I needed to know my freezer was
full, however, it wasn't. I wanted my cupboard full of clothes for the
winter . . . (actually I have found there is always room for more!) I
wanted my pantry stocked and all my children's needs supplied well in
advance. I needed to know that all these provisions would be met ahead
of time.

I wonder what situation Habakkuk was facing when he wrote these verses.
He had no figs, (can you imagine living without figs), no grapes, no
produce, no cattle, none of the staples considered necessities of life, and
yet, he was rejoicing.

Deep inside I know He places us in these difficult times. He causes us to
rejoice in the fact that He alone is our God and Provider. He Faithfully
designs circumstances that teach us to trust at all times and in every

way. He daily reminds us that He is the source of our every need. Our seeming lack becomes His opportunity to bestow His never-ending supply. Sometimes, one day at a time.

I was reminded of being in that place once before. There is a story I love to tell. It's a simple story, not profound like so many I could tell concerning His provision. However, it reflects how our Father meets His children in the everyday needs and desires of their lives.

I woke up one morning and prepared to have a bubble bath with my favorite scent, however, there was very little left in the container. Feeling somewhat annoyed, I drained the bottle dry. I can remember not enjoying that bath very much. I was too busy pouting, sulking and hosting a pity party held entirely in my honor! After all, what is life when you can't afford bubble bath!

I somewhat reluctantly finished my bath, put on my housecoat and went downstairs. When I reached the bottom step I felt a chill coming from our front door and noticed it had been left slightly open. Wondering why, I opened the door and noticed a large bag tucked inside. Someone had obviously wanted to leave something for us without being identified.

When I opened the bag . . . can you guess what I found? It was a huge bottle of my favorite bubble bath; the very one I had just run out of. My Faithful God was there. There were also His people who at His bidding delighted in delivering His surprise packages.

I have to admit this journey of trust is not always the easiest to embark upon. In fact, it seems to be in direct conflict with our human nature. You see total trust causes us to live one day at a time . . . indeed there are times it is one moment at a time. It is natural to want to plan, and provide for ourselves days and even years in advance. However, there are times our Heavenly Father has other plans for His children. He sits enthroned in the Heavens watching the striving and worrying that accompanies our daily schedule. He who holds this entire universe in the palm of His hand wants to remind His children that He is indeed able to provide for you. Sometimes the journey may seem difficult, however, be assured that you are His responsibility. His to feed, clothe and provide for. Remember He too walked this earth. He too had physical needs. However, He had complete trust in Him who is our source.

There is some wonderful counsel left to us in the book of Matthew. In the few short years that He walked among us there were some definite truths He needed to convey. You see trust is a timeless issue, however, provision is timeless as well . . .

Listen to His words . . .

"Therefore I tell you, do not worry about your life, what you will eat or drink; or about your body, what you will wear. Is not life more important than food, and the body more important than clothes? Look at the birds of the air; they do not sow or reap or store away in barns, and yet your heavenly Father feeds them. Are you not much more valuable than they? Who of you by worrying can add a single hour to his life? And why do you worry about clothes? See how the lilies of the field grow. They do not labor nor spin. Yet I tell you that not even Solomon in all his splendor was dressed like one of these. If that is how God clothes the grass of the field, which is here today and tomorrow is thrown into the fire, will he not much more clothe you, O you of little faith? So do not worry, saying, 'What shall we eat?' or 'What shall we drink?' or 'What shall we wear?' For the pagans run after all these things, and your heavenly Father knows that you need them. But seek first his kingdom and his righteousness, and all these things will be given to you as well. Therefore do not worry about tomorrow, for tomorrow will worry about itself."

Matthew 6:25-34

I find my heart once again saying 'yes Lord' . . .
Habakkuk traveled this path . . .
I'm going once again . . .
I'll meet you on the heights . . .

* * * *

I Love Jesus

A DELIGHTFUL INHERITANCE 29

"I came into this world with nothing . . .
And so far I've been able to retain most of it!"

"Lord you have assigned me my portion and my cup;
you have made my lot secure.
The boundary lines have fallen for me in pleasant places;
surely I have a delightful inheritance."
Psalm 16:5

I have found comfort in this Psalm many times during my life and ministry. I find satisfaction in knowing that the Lord is my inheritance and my portion.

The Word tells us the Tribe of Levi, the Priestly Tribe, knew this to be truth as well. These Israelites were not given an allotment of land along with the other tribes who crossed over into the Promised Land. Instead, they were told that the Lord alone was to be their Inheritance. Being part of the 'Ministry Tribe' myself, I often wonder how they felt about this news. Now I don't know about you, but being as carnal as I am at times, I enjoy having at least a little something to call my own! Lets face it, owning property or a home feels good! It brings security, a sense of belonging and continuity to our lives.

I must confess I have been challenged many times in ministry as I have longed for a permanent place to call home! I long for roots, lifelong friends, family around the corner and most of all a homestead. The very thought of this brings visions of pleasure and security to my heart. However, once again our Lord steps into my dreams and agendas. He purifies my wants and desires and like a faithful and loving Father speaks clearly to my heart.

He reminds me that where my heart is so shall my home be. He causes me to rest in the knowledge that He alone is my Inheritance. His Word assures me that even now He is preparing my Homestead and those boundary lines can never be shaken regardless of where this physical body finds itself!

We had a loss recently. My husband's father, a Pastor of 50 years, went on to claim his Homestead. There was not a lot in terms of a physical inheritance, however, there was a strong spiritual heritage passed on to my husband, my children, and hopefully generations to come.

Why do we as humans equate the word 'Inheritance' with the temporal, the physical, and the monetary?

It's not.

God's inheritance to us is delightful.

For, He promises Himself.

* * * *

I Love Jesus

THE
FENCE

30

I never did like that fence! It wasn't ours of course. It was on the property of the people who lived across the street and two houses down from us.

Although I had an extreme dislike for that fence, I certainly understood the owner's motivation for building it. They lived on a large corner lot with absolutely no privacy. This fence however would have given shelter to Fort Knox . . . it was huge!

That fence provided a constant source of anxiety for me, as there was an abandoned railway line and an empty field on the other side of the fence where my little boy loved to play. There was also a road alongside the field on which our children traveled back and forth to school. My problem lay in the fact that I could not see a thing beyond that fence. I would watch as Justin walked down the street and disappeared behind that massive wall of painted wood. Sometimes he would walk on the railway ties. I liked that. It enabled me to watch the top of his little blond curls bounce their way down the field. However, the fence would eventually hide him from my view. Once around that corner he was gone from my sight.

That was very difficult for me. I am a MOTHER, an overprotective one at that! I wanted to know where my child was and how he was doing. I needed to know he was safe, and knowing Justin as I did, actually heading in the direction of school! There were times I would run upstairs to the second floor of our home hoping for a better view of my child and a few more seconds of security. I followed this routine twice a day, both to and from school. Always watching, waiting for that familiar face to make it's way around the fence.

It was nerve racking, as Justin was almost always last! Dozens of children would make their way around the fence while I waited for the face that I so longed to see. Thankfully he did find his way home, his little face eventually came into view and mother could relax again, for a little while!

We have long since moved from that city and from that home. I believe the fence still remains. I know the lessons are ongoing . . .

In spite of it's constant aggravation, the Lord used that fence in my life. As I would sit in my living room watching and waiting, I would hear Him whisper those very familiar words . . . "TRUST ME". They would bring a measure of peace to my heart, however, I would remind the Lord it was a very difficult thing to do, I couldn't see my child. The obstacle was too high. His voice always responded so clearly . . . "I CAN".

'Trust' . . . such a small word . . . such a huge endeavor. It would have been easier to drive my child to school every day, however, I knew in doing that I would never completely learn the lessons He wanted to teach me, and still does . . .

I confess there are times I find it very difficult to let go. I'm quite sure there are others who feel the same way. We hold on tightly, wanting and needing to control our circumstances and our environment. We fear the unknown. We become anxious over what is not clearly visible and understandable. When familiarity grows dim we try anything and everything to re-capture what we have always known. When we cannot see ahead, when large seemingly massive circumstances block all hope from view we become tempted to take matters into our own hands. We sit in agony worrying about that, which remains unknown and unseen.

The answer lies in trust. Fences teach that. Obstacles ultimately prove His power to supersede any seemingly impossible circumstance. They become a necessary part of our growth, a tool to develop trust.

I am reminded of that popular story many of us learned as small children. The story of that massive, seemingly unbeatable giant named Goliath. He stood in all his power and might, bestowing fear and intimidation on anyone who dared to challenge him. What Goliath had not counted on however, was that confidence and trust are always stronger weapons than fear and doubt. Standing in the shadow of this giant was a young shepherd boy who dared to place his confidence in One who overshadowed even the mightiest of mortal men. With merely a slingshot and a small pebble, the supposed indestructible giant was defeated.

David knew the source of his strength. Life had already proven to this young man that his God was greater than any other power. His trust, coupled with the strength and protection of the Almighty became an unbeatable force.

There is a song the Lord would remind me of when Justin was just a little boy, when he was out of my sight and hidden by that fence. I still sing it when I find myself anxious for my children or my circumstances. I need to hear its words when fear and doubt threaten to wind their way into my heart.

Maybe you find yourself where I have been.

You can't see ahead, circumstances obstruct your view . . .

You stand in the shadow of what appears to be greater than your ability to defeat . . .

Let me sing to you today . . .

"Why should I be discouraged
Why do the shadows fall
Why does my heart feel lonely and long for heaven and home
For Jesus is my portion
My constant Friend is He
For His eye is on the Sparrow
And I Know He watches me
For His Eye is on the Sparrow
And I Know He Watches me . . . (and Justin)

I sing because I'm happy
I sing because I'm free
For His Eye is on the Sparrow
And I Know He watches me" . . . (and Allyssa)
-Civilla D. Martin & Charles Hutchinson Gabriel

His Word promises that His eye **IS** on the Sparrow . . .

I also know with certainty . . .

His eyes are on **you** . . .

"Are not two sparrows sold for a copper coin?
And not one of them falls to the ground apart from your Father's will."
"But the very hairs of your head are all numbered."
"Do not fear therefore; you are of more value than many sparrows."
Matthew 10:29-31

* * * *

I Love Jesus

SCARS

31

*"A Religion that Gives Nothing,
Costs Nothing, Suffers Nothing . . .
Is Worth Nothing."*
        - -Martin Luther King

I remember so well the excitement of going to Summer Camp! The very words were alive with meaning! For a teenage girl it meant a week full of adventure, fun and most importantly . . . **BOYS!**

My friend Margaret and I were going together. That was nothing new; we were never far apart, as Margaret loved fun and adventure almost as much as I did!

We were both around the age of sixteen this one particular summer, both looking for a little romance! There was a major problem however, an embarrassing deterrent. I had the biggest ugliest wart you ever saw clearly visible on my left hand just below my thumb. Back then I had absolutely no problem turning most heads, however, what if one of those heads I'd turned wanted to hold my hand! They would think they had picked up a creature from the lily pond! They'd be afraid to kiss me. I'd be the reverse of all the fairy tales they had ever heard and turn into a toad right before their eyes!

Margaret and I knew we had to do something about this situation. We had no time for slow working medicines or chemicals . . . camp was upon us! Putting our heads together we came up with the most obvious solution, we decided to pick it off ourselves! I realize this was very silly and I certainly would not recommend this treatment for anyone suffering from this tragic disease. We did however pick away until the ugly lump was removed.

I really don't know why we did such a thing. Vanity definitely superseded common sense, as this process was extremely painful! I have proof . . . to this day I have a very large scar on my left hand. A reminder of what was once there.

I am older now. Wiser I hope. However, the years and the journey have left some blemishes and scars of their own. They are the visible memories and reminders of the bumps and bruises of this life.

We carry scars on our hearts as well.

There is one I will always remember, both for the pain, and for the healing . . .

I was in my mid-twenties. I'd lost a child. After returning from the hospital I lay in our bedroom and shook with the sobs only another mother who has lost a child can fully understand. The body that once carried, nurtured and loved a little life was now empty and silent. The life was gone. The dream had vanished.

In my desperation I cried aloud to the Lord. I feared I would forever carry this pain in my heart . . . forever bear the scars. It was then I heard His voice as clearly as I have ever heard it before. I heard Him whisper that He would turn every scar I carried into a mark of beauty. Gone would be the painful stain. He would replace it with beauty, growth of character, and a love that would touch the world around me. It was a wonderful exchange. I gave Him my scars . . . He gave me His beauty.

The Prophet Isaiah must have heard His whisper long before I did. He words it so wonderfully . . .

> *". . . to bestow on them a crown of beauty instead of ashes,*
> *the oil of gladness instead of mourning,*
> *and a garment of praise instead of a spirit of despair.*
> *They will be called oaks of righteousness,*
> *a planting of the Lord*
> *for the display of his splendor."*
> *Isaiah 61:3*

I am reminded that our Lord bore scars on His precious body. Those scars purchased our redemption and made the exchange possible. Heaven will be a delight as we look upon the hands, feet and side of Jesus. You see, we will know Him by those scars. They are evidence of His wounds while on His journey; ultimately they speak of His willingness to identify with us . . . to take our pain upon Himself.

I remember many times as a young child tearfully handing over a broken toy or favorite treasure to my dad. To my young mind, there was nothing beyond his ability to fix. Time after time, my trust in him was rewarded as he handed me my treasure perfectly restored.

I encourage you to do the same with our Heavenly Father . . . the One who is the Redeemer and Restorer of our broken hearts.

Give Him your scars and make the exchange.

He will give you Beauty for Ashes . . . Beauty Marks for Scars

There is a song I have loved to sing since I was a very small child . . .

Let me sing it to you . . .

"I shall Know Him
I shall Know Him
As Redeemed by His side I shall stand.
I shall Know Him
I shall Know Him
By the prints of the nails in His hands."

* * * *

I Love Jesus

MASKS 32

Have you ever returned home after being away for a very long, long, time? I'm not referring to parents and family, but rather, the neighborhood, school or church where you grew up. Maybe you have recently attended a high school reunion. If you did, I'm wondering if you experienced the same emotions I did. I'm almost willing to bet you behaved better!

The church I grew up in recently celebrated an anniversary. In my teens I had sang in a trio and we were now being invited back to be the special music for this celebration. A wonderful weekend had been planned with some very special guests including our denominations national leader, many former pastors and friends and a well-known author and speaker. I was looking forward to seeing my friends again, I was also anxious to impress! This however was going to require some work on my part!

I have a friend named Linda who had also returned home for the celebrations. We were getting ready for the banquet on Saturday afternoon when she suggested I try enhancing the look of my hands by wearing false nails! Of course I was game. I'd never had nice nails in my life and I was sure everyone would be impressed to see my hands looking so elegant and beautifully manicured!

This was not to be the case. Disaster struck. My beautifully manicured nails began to fall off just before our names were announced to sing. Fortunately, Linda was seated at our table and had brought along glue just in case such an emergency arose. We very quickly tried to repair the damage.

I stuck the nail on my finger and then placed my nail between my teeth to hold it firmly in place. I couldn't believe what happened next . . . the fake nail stuck to my upper lip! You may laugh now, however I can assure you I was in panic mode! My nails were falling off, one was stuck to my lip, and my name was about to be announced. To make matters worse, the dignitaries were seated directly in front of the spot where I would be standing. What an impression I was about to make!

I finally managed to pry the nail off my lip but had no time to glue the rest back on. When our name was announced I tried to calm myself and walk somewhat serenely to the platform. However, another crisis occurred . . .

My dress had only three buttons on the front that held it together. The bottom one fell off just as I stood. There I was home after twenty years with my nails half on half off, and my dress falling apart. Instead of beautifully manicured nails holding a microphone for all to see, ridiculous looking nails clung tightly to the front of my dress hoping to keep myself decent and together! If that weren't enough, I still had patches of glue on my upper lip. I wanted to run out the back door and never come home again!

What a picture I made. It was not quite the one I had anticipated and hoped for, however, that's what happens when we wear masks . . . they often fall off.

What is it about human nature?

What is this incredible drive in us to appear to be something that in truth we are not?

Why is it so necessary for us to impress others, to have people extol our appearance and talent?

I fear we have become confused and lost our perspective. We have bought into the lie that claims our worth lies in our outside appearance, the external and visible qualities that we possess. As a result, we often neglect what is valuable to our God, and ultimately, ourselves.

The truth is, I have spent many years cultivating my character, and seeking after that which would make me more like the one I call 'Lord'. In my desire to impress I temporarily forgot what was important. I ignored the very things that would draw my friends to me once again. I saw only the imperfect in my life and desired by any means to cover it up.

110

That's what masks do. They hide who and what we really are. It's such a relief when they come off, such freedom not to carry their awkward weight. It is only then our true self can be visible. However, that's where the work really begins! These changes are not achieved through glue and tinsel, but rather a close and intimate walk with the Lover of our Souls.

I have changed over the years. It is my hope and desire to continue this process. In the mean time, I want my friends to see the real me. More importantly, I want them to see Jesus.

There is a chorus I love to sing that has been around for many, many years. It is still significant today.

Looking back, it would have been an appropriate choice for that evening . . .

"Let the Beauty of Jesus be seen in Me
All His Wonderful Passion and Purity
Oh Thou Spirit Divine
All My Nature Refine
Till the Beauty of Jesus be seen in me."
-G.L. Johnson & C. Derricks

* * * *

I Love Jesus

THE COMPETITION

33

*"How far you go in life depends on your being tender with the young,
compassionate with the aged, sympathetic with the striving,
and tolerant of the weak and the strong.
Because some day in life you will have been all of these."*
George Washington Carver

I have a brilliant sister named Geri. Geri and I being the closest in age shared a room off and on during our growing up years. As happens in most families, we were branded and stereotyped. I was the full of life and outgoing child . . . Geri was smart!

Now, I must confess, I do have a few brains of my own! I actually did very well in school when it didn't interfere with my social schedule! Geri on the other hand loved to study. At night she would play a recorded tape of her lessons in order to digest the material even while she slept! I think I may have learned more during my sleep than I did during my waking hours however, they were Geri's lessons and not my own!

Geri and I had both studied piano with The Royal Conservatory of Music and were scheduled for our theory exam on the same day. Determined that for once I was going to get a better mark than Geri, my self-imposed competition began. I studied at every opportunity I could find becoming obsessed with the thought of surpassing this genius I shared a room with.

Examination day arrived along with its accompanying emotions. We took the subway to downtown Toronto where we began our exam in The Royal Conservatory of Music building. It had all the warmth of the city morgue. No smiles, no noise, no life at all! When the allotted time was over, we handed in our papers and headed home. I was happy, talkative, and very confident. Geri on the other hand was quiet and fearful she had made mistakes. I tried to assure her she probably had achieved perfection while inwardly hoping she hadn't!

Several weeks passed before the test results arrived by mail. Thankfully, Geri was not home when they were delivered as my confidence had completely vanished. I wondered if I had even managed to pass. With extreme nervousness and trepidation I opened my envelope, however, I looked at my mark and jumped for joy! It was INCREDIBLE! With the thrill of victory filling my entire being I now awaited Geri's homecoming and my long last opportunity to gloat!

Several hours passed before Geri arrived home. Being the private person she is, she quietly took her envelope to our room and opened it. Nothing was said. She remained calm while the suspense was killing me! Finally, she told us in her calm and collected way the mark she had received. If my mark had been <u>INCREDIBLE,</u> Geri's was definitely <u>MORE INCREDIBLE</u>! I couldn't believe it. She had beaten me once again. The competition that had consumed my life for so long was now over. However, the lesson's had just begun . . .

Life is full of competition. It can be a healthy and necessary tool in our lives, or a destructive weapon leaving those scarred by it with feelings of insecurity and unworthiness. In its worst form, consuming jealousy along with hatred and bitterness claim its victims

I love to tell the story of a race run at 'The Special Olympics' . . .

The race began . . . the children took off. Not long into the race however, one little boy lost his balance and fell. When the other children heard their fellow competitor crying they came running back to see what was wrong with him. The natural response would have been to keep going! With less to compete, surely victory was more attainable. This was not the case. Together the young boys picked up their fallen friend and arm in arm crossed the finish line as one united team. The competition was over. Winning had become irrelevant with the need of their friend becoming the greater goal.

Here we see that competition can be a wonderful force in our lives. When kept in perspective it will cause us to run along side each other pushing one another to be the best we can be. Like athletes we give each other something to strive for. Higher goals, broader visions, and new levels of confidence and determination are competitions healthy reward. Our priority does not lie in surpassing others abilities, but rather in obtaining new personal heights and breaking our individual records.

These are the good, the constructive sides of competition. However, this is not always the case. Competition when placed in the wrong context can become a destructive consuming force in the lives of those who become obsessed by it. It causes people to lose their own sense of identity and personhood as they strive to become like, and ultimately, better than others. Jealousy and covetousness become the motivating factors in their life. They cease to view people as fellow travelers on the road of life, rather, they become objects to beat and ultimately destroy.

I have witnessed this kind of destruction. So have you. I am reminded of the warning the Apostle Paul gave to the church in Philippi . . .

"Do nothing out of selfish ambition or vain conceit,
but in humility consider others better than yourselves."
Philippians 2:3

Strife tears down placing others below you. Vain glory lifts oneself up placing you above others. These responses however do not need to control our lives. We have been given the alternative. I believe the solution lies for all of us in complete acceptance, and ultimately, contentment with who God has created each one of us to be.

There is no other like me and there is no other like you. Our calling and gifting are unique. Individually we have much to offer. Corporately we become complete. It is in bringing our separate talent and abilities together that we can achieve so much more for ourselves and ultimately, more for the Kingdom.

We can run alongside each other, however, we need to realize that there will come a bend in the road with room for only one to run. Our paths will lead in different directions. One will not be a better path, one not worse. They will be different, unique and tailor-made for each traveler. Understand who <u>YOU</u> are.

Put jealousy behind you, as it will eventually destroy every wonderful positive quality you possess.

Don't strive to be like someone else . . . you will miss the most incredible gift other than the gift of His Son that God has given you.

Yourself!

* * * *

I Love Jesus

"WHO AM I?" 34

S ometimes life has a way of getting even with those of us who tend to have mischievous tendencies. . .

While attending college, I decided to audition for the school's vocal travel team. To my surprise and delight I was accepted and immediately started touring on weekends. I loved every aspect of this experience, however, there was a problem that cropped up every now and then . . .

There would come a point in every service where we would stop singing in order to introduce ourselves, tell where we were from and what year of study we were in. On more than one occasion, someone actually had the nerve to steal my name! I would stand in horror as I heard another girl, from another place; introduce herself as 'Heather Sheldon' from Toronto, Ontario. The microphone would then be passed to me where I would stand dumbstruck not knowing who I should be, or, where I had come from. Some who are not particularly attached to their names may not have a problem with this; I however am not one of those. I like my name; my identity is wrapped up in it and I am recognizable to others by it. My friends found my dilemma very amusing. I would have to, if it had happened to someone else!

The question of 'who am I', often arises in life as we try to carve a place for ourselves in this world. Many find their identities difficult to establish or even lost in the shadow of someone else! Some even adjust their personalities in order to fit or blend with whatever their surroundings may be.

I had actually entered Bible College to prepare for what I thought would be a lifetime of pastoral ministry. I grew up with a sense of calling on my life. Deep inside I knew I would end up married to a Pastor. My Pastor's Wife suspected this as well and worked hard trying to instill some sense of appropriate behavior in me. I was not the easiest student however. Life was too much fun to be worrying about such serious matters.

As a result I wondered how I would survive in this perfect world of 'pastoring'. I found myself looking with awe and reverence at minister's wives who in my perspective looked perfect and tidy in every way. They seemed so placid and calm. To my young mind they were definitely saint material!

I on the other hand did not fit this description. I knew I loved Jesus with all my heart. I knew I loved people and had much to offer. Quite frankly, I just didn't look or act the part! When I finally entered the hallowed halls of ministry I was left with a dilemma. I would either adapt my personality to my calling or, I would just try and fake it! The safest decision at the time seemed to be the latter.

I began to assume an 'alter ego' . . . a new improved Heather. I worked hard at matching the demeanor of those I perceived to be worthy mentors. Miserably I tried to walk instead of bounce. I adjusted my countenance to look calm and sophisticated and learned to smile ever so sweetly. My efforts were in vain however as my true personality was unable to be disguised. People saw beyond the superimposed image to the real me, the true Heather. I will ever remain grateful that they did.

In reality, we are all called to be an example. No matter who we are, or whom we surround ourselves by; we are all examples to someone! Here's where the problem lies . . . one cannot be an example or an influence on others if we are not comfortable with ourselves! I was a horrible example of the perfect ministers wife, but a wonderful influence when I offered people me! The good, the not so good, and the in between.

I have come to understand that is ultimately what people want. They want you and me just as we are, willing to be vulnerable, willing to be real, and most importantly, willing to be made more like Him. There is only one perfect example. He calls us to be like Himself, no other. A reflection of His character . . . sons and daughters desiring to grow up like their Father.

I very quickly threw away my silly expectations. Hopefully, I'll remain free of those impossible standards and endeavor to be an example of the best 'Heather' I can possibly be . . .

I heard a rather amusing quote the other day . . .

Allow me to share it with you . . .

"No person is absolutely unnecessary.
One can always serve as a horrible example."

* * * *

I Love Jesus

WEAKNESS 35

"But he said to me,
A My grace is sufficient for you,
for my power is made perfect in weakness."
Therefore I will boast all the more gladly about my
weaknesses,
so that Christ's power may rest on me.
That is why, for Christ's sake,
I delight in weaknesses, in insults,
in hardships, in persecutions, in difficulties.
FOR WHEN I AM WEAK,
THEN I AM STRONG."
2 Corinthians 12:9-10

Weakness is not considered an asset in this fast paced competitive world we live in. I often think of the bumper sticker I have seen as I drive down the highway . . . **"He who has the most toys when he dies wins!"**

Can you imagine people driven to achieve, driven to perform, driven to make enough money just so they have the title and appearance of a 'Winner'. Power, control, energy, aggression . . . these are all contemporary descriptions of strength. I believe however it is a sad commentary on our time causing me to wonder what history will record about our generation.

The Apostle Paul obviously chose another road other than the one I most often travel. Instead of bumper sticker philosophy he offered us his heart, his humanity, and his vulnerability. What an incredible contradiction. This great man actually took delight in hardships, persecution, insults and difficulties. In the natural this does not make sense. I can't imagine finding joy in an insult!

I remember all too well seasons of weakness in my life. Delight was not always a word I would use to describe those moments. I felt weak. Sickness had taken its toll. Young children and heavy responsibilities in ministry drained me of energy and strength. I struggled at times with worth questioning how I could be of value to the Lord when I felt so tired! I am no expert on the life and times of the Apostle Paul; however, in our society spirituality and weakness do not appear to dwell together. So often in contemporary preaching we are taught that for the Child of God everything will be positive. Winning battles, tackling the enemy and converting the world become signs of a strong believer!

I am so glad that His presence in my life has taught me differently. I wonder where contemporary Christianity went wrong? Have we read too many bumper stickers, or have we adapted well to the philosophy that surrounds us.

Like you, I have my hero's . . . people I admire and respect. When my children were younger two women who I never met had an incredible influence on my life. The example of their lives has served to confirm the truths I know God has been teaching me . . .

So many of us have heard the tragic story of Joni Eareckson, a beautiful and vibrant young girl who became injured in a diving accident. She was left crippled; unable to walk or function in ways so many of us take for granted. Yet, to me she is strong. I see strength and character in the words of her books. Most importantly, I see the heart and spirit of my Lord. Like the Apostle Paul has so beautifully stated, her weakness has become her strength. A strength that continues to portray the impact a surrendered vessel can bring to this world.

The story of Corrie ten Boom has also left a deep impact on my life. This incredible woman took the bitterness of her experience in a Nazi Prison Camp and gained from it a testimony of love and forgiveness that ultimately caused her voice to be heard around this entire world. From her bondage and captivity a supernatural grace and strength was birthed.

I love these verses. They bring us a reason to hope. **They instill a confidence that measures our worth on the ruler of His grace rather than the limits of our ability**. I know at times I'm weak, however I have learned that complete dependence on Him is what He requires. Total inability in our own strength enables His power to be at work within us.

The result of our efforts becomes so much more when His strength has perfected our own.

I have found the reality of these verses to be quite a paradox and definitely opposite to the mindset of our day, however, when given the choice, His strength and grace will always be greater than my own.

How about you?

Have feelings of weakness and inadequacy overwhelmed you?

Does your heart long for that which your physical body cannot endure?

Maybe you need a shift in your thinking . . .

Throw away the concepts of strength that keep you striving and performing . . .

Take a journey to the foot of the cross. Know that because your Saviour took upon Himself the pain and sins of this entire world, we can now walk in His enabling strength. Understand that in God's economy weakness is quite all right . . .

For when we are weak . . .

Then we are strong.

* * * *

I Love Jesus

YOU ARE SO BEAUTIFUL   36

"Shared Joy Equals Double Joy
Shared Sorrow Equals Half Sorrow."

Have you ever struggled with issues of worth?

Have you ever lost perspective and looked to others to find your affirmation and security?

Have you ever placed your identity in position, title, talent and material gain?

Chances are a resounding 'yes' would be the answer from almost every reader. There is a temptation to place our security and our identity in how others view us, or the title or position we may hold. Our worth often diminishes when circumstances cause us not to feel good about ourselves. If we were completely honest, we would remember times when unhappiness over our physical appearance or discontent with our talent and abilities caused us to loose perspective and become dissatisfied with who we are. We often transfer these feelings to how we believe God sees us. His viewpoint becomes lost and possibly distorted as we focus on the negative in our life.

I confess I was struggling yesterday! My perspective was completely lost as I wrestled with the timeless issue of worth! To make matters worse, I had to go to work that way! My fellow workers are familiar with a smiling cheerful Heather, so, I pasted on my best smile and endeavored to forget my troubles for a little while!

I tried to get about my business and deal with my customers when I heard a rather loud noise. It became obvious that someone was yelling, and, they were yelling at me! That was all I needed! When I turned around to see who it was, I was quite surprised. The woman was obviously mentally challenged (possibly Down Syndrome) in her late twenties, early thirties. I could not understand what she was saying but I knew others around her had understood and were watching for my response. I walked over and as kindly as I could asked her to repeat what she had just said to me.

Good and loud, for all to hear, she clearly yelled the words . . . **"YOU ARE SO BEAUTIFUL"**.

I melted. It was all I could do not to drop on the floor and start wailing right in front of everyone. I needed those words so badly that day. He knew I did. He sent her to me. It was His heart reminding mine of how He see's me. She spoke not with correctness of speech, flattering tongue or private motives. She spoke instead with simplicity, purity of heart, and innocence.

Immediately I felt . . . **BEAUTIFUL!!**

My Lord dealt with me all that day and well into the night. He was once again allowing the process of life and His presence in it to draw me closer to Himself. He was reminding me through the simplest of His vessels how He viewed me. He was communicating to me once again that His love for us is not based on our talents, appearance, title or any other external factor. His love for us goes beyond the surface and envelopes our entire being. It's amazing to understand that it is not a matter of being good enough with our Lord; rather, it is knowing that His beauty revealed through us, is always enough!

Once again I had a glimpse at the love of my Father's heart and understood that His love will transcend any negative thoughts that may come my way. . .

There is a love song my husband regularly sings to me.

You may have heard the words before . . .

"You are so beautiful to me.
You are so beautiful to me.
You're everything I hoped for.
You're everything I need.
You are so beautiful to me."

- Billy Preston & B. Fisher

I love it when he sings it to me.

I love it even better when Jesus sings it.

He sang it to me yesterday!

Listen as He sings it to you . . .

* * * *

I Love Jesus

127

STRETCHED 37

"Sing, O barren woman, you who never bore a child;
burst into song, shout for joy, you who were never in labor;
because more are the children of the desolate woman
than of her who has a husband, says the Lord.
Enlarge the place of your tent, stretch your tent curtains wide,
do not hold back; lengthen your cords, strengthen your stakes.
For you will spread out to the right and to the left;
your descendants will dispossess nations and settle in their
desolate cities."
Isaiah 54:1-3

I have found life to be full of 'stretching experiences' in every sense of the word! Allow me to share mine with you . . .

I have been having physiotherapy recently . . . a result of mid-life announcing itself to my poor body! My family doctor referred me to a local physiotherapist due to a disc problem in my lower back. Anxious for any type of relief, I quickly consented.

On one particular visit, he recommended we use 'traction' to pull the disc back in place. I had experienced this technique on a previous visit. I can assure you I cringed at the mention of its name. The physiotherapist did not seem to notice my hesitancy. Chatting away, he hooked me up to the horrible contraption, turned on the dreaded machine and left me to my misery. I laid face down, unable to move with all manner of hooks and belts around me. I felt like I was in a straight jacket.

I tried to think pleasant thoughts, anything to take my mind off my awkward, and I might add, embarrassing position! On this particular visit however we ran into a real problem. The machine didn't shut itself off! It somehow became jammed and continued to pull and stretch.

I couldn't believe what was happening! I tried to undo the belts however it was no use; I was tightly locked into place. In my mind I pictured scenes from all the horror movies I had watched as a child! Scenes of cruel villains putting their victims on the 'racks' raced through my mind. I am fairly tall now however a few more moments of that treatment and I would have been N.B.A. material!

I did what any normal 'stretched' person would do under the circumstances. With my poor body about to be pulled from it's joints, I began to scream and yell for help! The secretary on duty finally heard me and came running to my aid. I begged her not to put me through that horrible process again. My dignity had disappeared. I wanted out of that machine and I wanted out immediately! I realized I was not going to get my way when they began to hook me up to the dreaded machine. Making sure the equipment was set correctly, the process began once again.

In retrospect for anyone who was observing, it really was a funny scene. I did not find it amusing, however I realize the process was necessary for my healing . . .

It's what we all need.

It's what God desires to do in our lives.

He will allow circumstances in our life that cause us to be 'spiritually stretched'. His desire is to take us where we have never been before. Unfortunately, our extreme dislike of the process causes us to remain in our 'comfort zones'. As Isaiah has stated, we limit ourselves to 'tents'. We choose small confined places with defined boundaries that are often placed on property that does not belong to those dwelling in them.

I have learned God wants more for us. Indeed, He has promised more. His Word declares that we will spread to the right and to the left. The cities will be ours, and also, the nations.

This however involves a choice on our part. We must have a willingness to leave behind that which we have long outgrown. Instead of fear and uncertainty, maintain an attitude of expectancy along with a heart, soul and mind that are ready to be enlarged by Him.

I know at times its painful. It's much easier to remain in our 'comfort zones'. I rather like my own. However. I want everything that God has prepared for me. I want the fullness of His plan and calling for my life. I may yell and scream for help when I can take the stretching no longer. I may try all manner of contortions to free myself of my current bondage. However, I know He will be there . . . for all of us. He will come running to our aid and there He will remain until the process is complete. Till we are further equipped and ready for what He has ahead for us, and we are once again enlarged and ready for service.

Your Father may be stretching you even now . . .

What was once considered familiar and safe may have been removed from your life . . .

You may be experiencing uncertainty, and possibly even fear . . .

Know that this time has purpose . . .

In this process you once again will see . . .

Barrenness fading . . .

Service waiting . . .

Jesus remaining.

* * * *

I Love Jesus

THE FLOOD PLAIN

Apparently the city is constructing a Flood Plain just behind our back yard. Who would have thought such a pleasant sounding project could be so bothersome! The noise starts at sunrise and continues through till sunset.

Constant banging, trucks driving back and forth, whistles blowing, blasts of dynamite. It's enough to make a normally even tempered person a little edgy! Every morning I pray Godspeed for those construction men. In other words . . . "Lord, could you please hurry them along!"

There is one machine in particular that grates on all our nerves! It never stops. Twelve to fourteen hours a day it can be heard. I decided to check out what was causing this constant irritating clatter and made a discovery, which led me to the reason for its continual use. We live on very rocky ground. Just below the surface lies layer upon layer of rocky shale. This machine is used to drill holes through the rock in order to insert dynamite below the surface. After the explosion, the fragments are loaded onto a truck and disposed of.

I wasn't aware we lived on such rocky terrain. On the surface our area is very lovely. Green fields, beautiful mature trees, and a variety of growth that displays itself wonderfully surround us.

Once again I see the parallel to our lives, indeed our hearts. The surface appears great without a trace of rocky ground. On the outside we display the evidence of lush growth and fruitfulness. However, I am reminded of the One who is at work within us. He sees where no other can. His eyes view our deepest most intimate thoughts and intents. In His desire to refine and purify His children He begins to work in our hearts. His labors never cease. They take Him all through the day and continue through the night hours.

He allows circumstances in our lives knowing their impact will bring change to our hearts. He ordains situations that tenderize us. He takes the Word of God and the Sword of His Spirit and penetrates into the deepest, hardest, most hidden places, and then He begins to chip away. It is a slow process sometimes as the ground below the surface can become hardened through years of dormancy and neglect. It never stops Him though. He is determined to root from us all that causes us to be tough and unfit for service. He wants us tender, soft, vulnerable and willing to be like clay in His hands.

He does this in order to make us ready. As the plain behind my home is being prepared for storms and floods so He prepares us. He wants us ready for the floods, ready for the rain and storms of life. We will be a shelter to those who need a refuge from their own personal disasters. A place that absorbs the pain and tears that flow from lives with nowhere else to turn and a quiet stream where others come for refreshing.

It has certainly not been a pleasure living through all this construction behind me; however, I have the confidence I will witness something very beautiful when it is all complete.

I think I'll let them continue . . .

I will allow Him to as well. You would be wise to also. I know it's a seemingly slow and painful process, however, I believe the end result will be worth it, for all of us.

Continue Lord . . . chip away.

> *". . . BEING CONFIDENT OF THIS,*
> *THAT HE WHO BEGAN A GOOD WORK IN YOU*
> *WILL CARRY IT ON TO COMPLETION*
> *UNTIL THE DAY OF CHRIST JESUS. "*
> *PHILIPPIANS 1: 6*

* * * *

I Love Jesus

134

THE GARDEN

39

We phoned a friend the other day and as is custom for many busy households we got their answering machine. I find most answering machines annoying, however, being the creative person Henk is, it is a pleasure to listen to the messages he leaves.

I loved one of his recent ones. It went something like this . . .

> *"Hi. . . Are you having a rough time in your life?"*
> *"Are you feeling unfairly treated?"*
> *"Remember . . . even a flower has to go through a lot of dirt*
> *before it can blossom!"*

How appropriate . . . an incredible analogy.

I do so love the garden. I love to sit quietly and drink of all its beauty and splendor during the summer months.

I also enjoy watching the visitors that come to the garden. Some have even found a home there. Birds of all types and varieties, busy little squirrels and even a rabbit or two go about their daily routines in the garden. They are drawn to the lush beauty and vegetation it has to offer. A source of life for so many. A place of quietness and rest for others.

My father is an incredible gardener. I'm quite sure he can make anything grow . . . anywhere! I believe I have inherited his love for gardening, however, not his talent! My abilities take me to the greenhouse where I purchase the finished product of someone else's labor of love! They are then transplanted into my garden where I try and remember to water them every once in awhile!

I have been known however to buy some seeds and plant them in the early months of spring. I am like a child running outside almost daily to monitor the progress of my tiny seeds. It has never ceased to amaze me how such incredible beauty and variety can come from such a small, seemingly insignificant seed. It's a miracle really. However, the garden is a place of miracles, a place of life. A reflection of our God in all His splendor and creativity.

You see, from the conception of time itself the very lessons of life and death have been contained in the garden. The splendor and vitality that brings pleasure to so many is ultimately a result of death . . . death that bursts forth into life.

The Gospel of John explains it so clearly . . .

> *"I tell you the truth,*
> *unless a kernel of wheat falls to the ground and dies,*
> *it remains only a single seed.*
> *But if it DIES,*
> *it produces many seeds."*
> *John 12:24*

Our Lord was speaking of His own impending death, His life being the seed that would experience death in order for you and I to know life eternal. I believe however, He wanted to teach us more . . .

We need to come to the understanding that before we can blossom, before we bear fruit and multiply, we need to die to ourselves, our plans, our agendas, and ultimately, our will. Death is never easy. Our human nature fights for control. We want to carve out our own destiny, determine our own design, and finally, create our own finished product. This takes hard work! The mind must constantly be planning, scheming and fighting for control.

I have learned that though the process be painful, it is easier to die to myself and leave the work to the expert!

You see, our Heavenly Father is the Master Gardener. He cultivates the soil of our heart and tenderly nurtures the seed He has planted. He is daily pruning, cutting off that which affects our growth and beauty. He brings the Sun. He also allows the rain and storms. They are both necessary, both vital for our growth.

136

I know there are times the Sun on your face will only be a distant memory, your vision clouded by the weight that hangs over you. However, I know He is doing what every good gardener needs to do. He is allowing the seed to die that it may live again to blossom, to bear fruit, and eventually become a picture of beauty for all to behold. As in most gardens, visitors will be welcome. Some may even remain awhile. They will come to drink in quietly of the strength and beauty He will cultivate in your life.

The garden must change however. It needs to die frequently in order for the seasons to be fulfilled. We will experience our seasons as well. There will be times of abundant life and growth along with seasons of death and seeming darkness. They are all fruitful, all necessary. Seasons blending together to create the finished picture.

We need to remember our Father . . . the Master Gardener who is ever at work tilling the soil of your heart. He is moment by moment watching you, daily checking your progress. The sun will shine again although it may seem you are forever buried beneath the layers that so weigh you down.

There will be beauty along with a lush growth of character . . .

Life from death . . .

From the seed . . .

A flower.

* * * *

I Love Jesus

HEART
OF A MOTHER

40

"THE JOY OF MOTHERHOOD:
WHAT A WOMAN EXPERIENCES WHEN ALL THE CHILDREN
ARE FINALLY IN BED! "

I am the consummate 'Mother'. In fact, if you look up the word in the dictionary, my name may even appear as part of its definition! Of course, I have been called a few names from time to time, children reacting to my strong sense of motherhood! Words such as 'paranoid', 'overprotective', and 'worry wart' have been tossed my way. I prefer much nicer terms such as 'responsible', 'loving', and 'caring'.

We have recently been through the 'New Year's Experience'. Murray and I were left to celebrate on our own this year as our children, older now, had both gone off to their various functions and activities with their friends. It really is wonderful to see them so happy. Fulfilling to know they are carving out their own lives and enjoying themselves so completely. However, I remain a <u>MOTHER!</u>

Our son left in the early afternoon and informed us that he would not be home until 8:30 or 9:00 the next morning. He was celebrating with the church youth group who were all very responsible, however, being the 'concerned' person I am, I wanted details, and, lots of them!

My poor child! I pumped him for information till I knew exactly where he was going, what he would be doing, and, who would be driving him home. Justin just gave me his little smirk, kissed me on the cheek and said . . . "Love you Ma", "Happy New Year" and then he walked out the door. There I stood wishing I could go with him, remembering when he was tiny and always by my side.

I actually didn't do too badly this year. Throughout the night I was fine, however, my most difficult time is when I am anticipating his imminent return. I sit by the window. I watch the clock. My activities never take me far from a spot where I can watch the car pull into the driveway.

As usual this morning I followed my routine watching, waiting and anticipating. Finally he walked through the front door and mom could relax once again! My child had returned. He was home, and more importantly, he was safe.

He was tired, but not too tired for his mom! He gave me his usual "Hi Ma", "Love You", "I'm Home". This time he threw in "Happy New Year" and " Good Night". Off to bed he went. I couldn't help myself, when I knew he would be sound asleep, I peeked in on my 6'3" giant, my child. I stood at his door encompassed by the nurturing feelings that accompany motherhood. Once again I realized that no matter the size or age, the overwhelming feelings of love for those God has placed in our care would always remain. I found incredible satisfaction in the fact that my child laid contented and safe under the care of his parent's roof.

My thoughts take me to another parent who through different circumstances also watched for the return of a son. . .

It seems to be a timeless issue . . . parents searching the horizon for a glimpse of their child. This child however, left under extremely negative conditions. Desiring an existence independent of His Father, he took his inheritance and left to pursue life on his own terms. Concern for his parents would appear to be the last thing on this child's agenda. Rather, in complete abandonment of all that was familiar He began a lifestyle quite opposite to that which he had known.

We know the story of the prodigal son so well. This wandering child very quickly squandered his inheritance on a questionable lifestyle that left him destitute and homeless. While living in the company of animals, the Word of God tells us his thoughts returned to the comfort and security of his home. Devising words of repentance and remorse, he makes plans to return to his father. Not as a son, but rather, a slave.

What has always captured my attention is the stance of the Father. Listen to Luke's account of this incredible man . . .

" But while he was still a long way off,
his father saw him and was filled with compassion for him;
he ran to his son, threw his arms around him and kissed him."

(Luke 15:20)

I can only begin to imagine the pain and suffering of this Father. I'm quite sure feelings of guilt and self-incrimination crossed his mind. There were probably questions concerning his efforts as a parent . . . did I do the right thing . . . did I love enough . . . could I have changed anything. In spite of circumstances, this loving father never abandoned his post. You see, his post wasn't at home comfortably waiting for a servant to announce his son's return. Neither was it some far off country where he enjoyed life as a now semi empty-nester. Rather, his post remained where he could watch for the return of his son. Faithfully he remained on guard till his eyes focused on the familiarity of a much-loved face.

My thoughts travel once again to the one I call 'Father'. There are times His children leave the safety and comfort of His loving presence. There are times we squander our inheritance, gifts and treasures on worldly desires and pleasure. How often while living in the filth and degradation of sinful lifestyles do our thoughts return to that which we chose to leave behind? Contrite and broken in spirit we return only to find that He too never left His post. His eyes continue to scan the horizon waiting for that familiar voice to call out their Father's name. Returning to His waiting arms we find ourselves welcomed home once again, not as a slave, but rather, a child.

I am reminded there will be a day I will come home to my Father forever. I'll joyfully greet Him and tell Him how much I love Him. I know He'll welcome me and return my words of love. Upon my arrival I will hear Him speak the words "Well done my child, welcome home, now enter into your rest". All those years of traveling the roads of life will finally be over. With contentment and an overwhelming sense of peace and security we will lay our heads on our Father's breast and know what it is like to finally arrive Home.

I know our Father will share our joy. He has long waited for that moment when He will finally gather His children to Himself safe in His kingdom that knows no end. Prodigals returned, children safe, parent's hearts at rest.

Unlike this mother, there will be no need for peeking . . .

We'll be by His side . . .

Forever.

* * * *

I Love Jesus

THE
HOLY CITY **41**

Then I saw a new heaven and new earth,
for the first heaven and the first earth had passed away, and there was no
longer any sea.
I saw a Holy City, the new Jerusalem, coming down out of heaven from God,
prepared as a bride beautifully dressed for her husband.
And I heard a loud voice from the throne saying,
"Now the dwelling of God is with men, and he will live with them.
They will be his people, and God himself will be with them and be their God.
He will wipe away every tear from their eyes.
There will be no more death or mourning or crying or pain,
for the old order of things has passed away."

Most young girls spend hours dreaming of the day they walk down the aisle into the arms of their perfect Prince Charming. We plan the ideal gown, beautiful bouquets, a church full of friends and family, and a romantic honeymoon in some exotic paradise. We begin our fairy tale existence with our handsome prince carrying us over the threshold into our own private castle where one day an army of adorable little children will fill our happy home. The fairy tale grows brighter with each glimpse of a possible prince, till one day the perfect candidate arrives and forever sweeps us off our feet and into our dreams . . .

Our dreams rarely take us beyond this point. Our childhood fantasies never include financial difficulties, sick children, and a prince that more closely resembles the overstuffed pumpkin! And the glass slipper from the fairy tale we love so much becomes lost not through some romantic endeavor, but rather, because the house is so messy we can't find it! Somehow however, through the day-to-day journey of life, our dreams live on . . .

It was quite an experience when my husband brought me to our first home. We were the Assistant Pastors at a church in Brockville Ontario; a lovely city nestled along the coastline of the St. Lawrence River. Murray told everyone in the congregation that his desire was to find us a home on the waterfront. People laughed at him, telling him it was impossible as the cost would be exorbitant, especially for a brand new pastor and his young wife. Murray however refused to give up his search. He had also planned and prepared for his dreams. He too had bright hopes for the future. He longed to provide a home for his new bride that would fulfill the desires of both their hearts.

Through rather miraculous circumstances, my husband was told about a little waterfront home available for rent at next to nothing! It was with joy and pride that he carried me over the threshold to begin our life together in that beautiful little home! I'm sure the look on my face made all his efforts worthwhile! My home was perfect, beyond what I ever could have imagined to begin my new life as a bride.

My thoughts take me once again to another day and another place. There were other dreams that filled my heart when I was a young child. As do most children, thoughts of what lay beyond our everyday existence often challenged my young mind. Fortunately, I had been introduced to the lover of my soul at a very young age. I was raised hearing stories on the wonders of His kingdom where golden streets, gates of pearl, and the brilliance of His face giving light to that glorious city captivated my heart and mind. I dreamed of a home that lay far beyond what I could feel and sense in the here and now.

He also captivated my heart. The Prince of Peace, the One who out of His love for me sacrificed the wonders of His kingdom to become like us. Such love became impossible to resist . . . His promises impossible to ignore. His betrothal included laying down His life for me. My dowry became my heart, my love and my lifetime commitment.

The future now lies before all of us . . .
The proposal has been made . . .
The Home prepared . . .
The Groom's hand extended . . .

There will come a day when together we will stand in awe and gaze at the beauty of our new Home as it descends from the heavens. Majesty and beauty far beyond even the greatest of our dreams will captivate our hearts forever. This earth with it's temporal pleasures and pain will fade away. Crying, death and mourning will be forever replaced with laughter and eternal joy. The distance between this life and the next will fade as our God makes His Home among us.

It's good to read these verses. It's necessary to understand that far beyond what you and I experience in this world, there is coming another day, another place . . .

A place where every dream and desire will be fulfilled in a place called Home . . .

Our heart says come Lord Jesus . . .

Your Bride waits . . .

* * * *

I Love Jesus

OPEN DOORS

42

"What he opens no one can shut,
and what he shuts no one can open."
Revelation 3:7

We woke to the sound of the phone ringing early one morning.
I was pregnant . . . again.

I say again because our son Justin was just a few months old and this
pregnancy was not something we would have chosen at that point in our
lives. It had been a tough year and I didn't feel prepared to go through
the demands of another pregnancy and a brand new baby.

Like most expectant mothers my body signaled get out of bed and get to
the bathroom. Murray ran to answer the phone and I to the washroom.
As I listened to his conversation I heard him say the word 'Alliston'. I
wondered where Alliston was, why were they calling us, and why so
early in the morning!

We were the Assistant Pastors at a church in the city of Guelph, Ontario
at the time. We absolutely loved ministering in that city, yet, were wondering if it was time for us to strike out on our own. I wondered if this
was a church interested in talking with us about the position of Senior
Pastor.

My wondering was cut short as with shock I noticed I was bleeding. I
was very frightened and upset however, I waited until Murray was finished his conversation before I gave him the horrible news. We very
quickly got dressed and drove to the Hospital.

I was well into my pregnancy and although not planned for this baby
was already dearly loved. I will never forget the compassion of our
family doctor. It was with tears in his eyes that he told us we would lose
this child. The process was not a quick one. It lasted for two very pain-

ful, anxious days. It was late into the second day that the Specialist was brought in to inform us there was no hope. It was time to do surgery.

I remember so clearly being ushered into the Operating Room. I was experiencing all the emotions that accompany any trip to the operating room, most of all I felt an incredible sense of loss. In spite of the circumstances, coming out of anesthetic proved to an experience I will never forget. I found myself on Holy Ground. Verses I had never heard before began pouring out of my mouth. I'm sure the recovery room staff wondered what had invaded their quietness.

The verse I seemed to be repeating most often was this one found in Revelation . . . **"What He opens no one can shut, and what He shuts no one can open."** I don't ever recall hearing or reading this verse before, however, when I got home and settled I looked up the verse and found it in the book of Revelation chapter three.

During this whole process Alliston had been the last thing on my mind, in fact, I probably didn't give it any thought at all. However, I knew that somehow through this verse God was speaking to us, and, I knew He was calling us to Alliston.

Several years after our arrival, the church had grown and was thriving in every way. Our present location did not meet the needs of our growing assembly, as a result, property was purchased and in two phases we built a beautiful new building.

In planning for our dedication service we decided to invite the General Superintendent of our denomination to be our guest speaker. I will never forget him standing behind that pulpit and announcing that God had led him to a scripture and theme for the dedication of our new building. That morning his theme was from Revelation chapter three . . . **"I will open a door that no man can shut."**

He wasn't there when I came out of surgery quoting that verse years before.

He didn't know I'd lost my baby but birthed a vision.

God knew because he was there.

He gives his Word and in His time He confirms it.

We so often hear that famous quote . . . 'When God shuts a door, He opens a window'. Windows of ministry were opened for us in that place called 'Alliston'. However the windows of heaven opened that day as well. They welcomed a little child that had taken an early flight Home. Many years have passed since that day; yet, I know there will be another dedication day. A day when we will stand before the Throne of God and be re-united with all those who have gone before us. I believe I will also see standing before me the fruit of those ministry years in that city.

Everyone of us will one day pass through that door that separates time from eternity . . . a door that once He opens for us we will remain in His presence time without end. Our time on this planet is really but a short breath compared to the vastness of eternity. While here however, we have been given a choice. There seems to be a plethora of doors that beckon us to enter. However, not every door opens to life. . . some doors lead to pain, heartbreak and eventually separation from God.

Today He stands at the door of your heart and He knocks, and He waits.

The choice remains yours . . .

The door remains open . . .

The Father waits . . .

* * * *

I Love Jesus

BORDER CROSSING 43

My mother is usually not the mischievous type. I lived most of my life with a fairly 'normal' mother; however on one of our trips to Florida I caught a glimpse of her more daring side. Unfortunately, it was at my expense.

We were only a few hours from home and had arrived at the border crossing between the United States and Canada. As we had spent money on gifts and souvenirs we needed to go through Customs in order to declare our purchases. Not interested in this process I headed to the washroom and left my mother to deal with the Customs Officials. In retrospect my lack of interest cost me dearly for after I was out of sight my mother and her allies devised their terrible plan.

I returned to find a very serious and intimidating young officer conversing with my Mom. He asked me my name and proceeded to tell me I matched the description of a young girl who had been smuggling drugs over the border. This was very serious. He told me I was to be taken into custody where all my belongings would be searched and possibly confiscated. If proven guilty, I would be detained in the United States where I would be tried and sentenced. Crossing the border to my home was no longer a possibility.

I was terrified. My fear became evident as immediately I began to imagine the worst possible scenario. I pictured unjust trials with false witnesses along with years of separation from family and friends sitting in some lonely jail cell. I couldn't believe this was happening to an innocent God-fearing girl like myself! More importantly, I didn't understand my mother's silence. Why didn't she tell them I was a good girl, innocent and incapable of this crime! She remained silent however . . . my antici-pated defence was withheld!

The plot did not last long. It couldn't. Unable to contain their laugher at my terrified response, my mother and her fellow conspirators finally confessed their guilt. There are no words to describe the relief I felt at that moment. I felt like someone who had just been released from the worst nightmare possible. The joy that accompanied my pardon defi-nitely overruled any other emotion I had been feeling. I was safe at last. Having been acquitted of all crime, the officials could detain me no longer. I was allowed to cross the border and head for my home.

When I think of the events of that day my mind often travels to another time and another place. I am reminded of the day when you and I will approach our final destination, our final crossing. There will be only One we need answer to and I joyfully anticipate His approach. I do not fear this encounter as I have learned that He is indeed able to keep us from falling. He is daily correcting and guiding our steps in order that we walk in holiness and purity before Him. His ultimate desire is to prepare us for our Final Destination.

With this incredible assurance I now walk into eternity with hope and confidence. I know that when I arrive at that final border crossing where time and eternity meet, He will guide me safely over. He will secure my passage. I'll be Home. It is there I will be presented with joy before the very Throne of God, spotless and blameless, innocent of all wrong.

The One who knows me best will gladly proclaim that He has indeed cleansed every blemish and I will stand clothed in His righteousness. I will be welcomed with great joy to my eternal home, never again to leave its safety and comfort. The bondage of this world and the prison of the enemies' plans will hold me no longer. Instead of separation I look forward to wonderful reunion with those who have made the crossing before me.

I know my declaration will not be one of trinkets and souvenirs, but rather praise and worship to our God.

I look forward to standing together with you exclaiming with joy and gratitude . . .

**" . . . to the only God our Saviour be glory, majesty,
power and authority through Jesus Christ our Lord,
before all ages, now and forevermore."**

* * * *

I Love Jesus

IN THE FULNESS OF TIME

44

There is no doubt in my mind the winds of God are blowing. His love, power, and grace are being manifest across this entire planet. Stories of revival and conversions regularly encourage our faith.

We need not be shocked nor frightened for He is doing exactly as He promised. He is visiting us. Fresh waves of His incredibly rich presence are being poured out on the heart ready to receive.

Recently my husband and I along with other members of the church we were pastoring made a very long trip. Hundreds of thousands of people have made the same journey. We like the wanderers of old desired to see what God was doing in that particular place. We were not disappointed. It was an awesome experience. Our hearts were deeply touched as we witnessed hundreds of people making the decision to surrender their lives to Jesus Christ.

There was a cost however. For most the journey was long, and once the destination was reached, the waiting had just begun. Everyday hundreds of people lined the parking lot patiently waiting, eagerly anticipating, obviously longing.

Somehow I believe that is what He wants for all of us, everywhere, <u>ALL THE TIME</u>. Many cannot make the physical journey, however, that really is not important. He calls each of us to make this journey in our hearts, and once we arrive, to wait.

My mind wanders to the examples left to us in the Word of God. I think of Anna the prophetess who when widowed at a young age turned her grief into worship and followed her heart to the Temple. The Word indicates that Anna believed in the One who was to come. The Promised Child who would bring redemption to His people. As a result, the years found her watching, waiting and praying. Her heart remained steadfast in her desire to see the Messiah.

As was custom for the day, Mary and Joseph took their infant child to be presented at the Temple. It was there that Anna's tired and aging eyes finally gazed with wonder on His face.

Listen to what Luke tells us about this incredible woman . . .

> *"There was also a prophetess, Anna,*
> *the daughter of Phanuel, of the tribe of Asher.*
> *She was very old;*
> *she had lived with her husband seven years after her marriage,*
> *and then was a widow until she was eighty-four.*
> *She never left the Temple but worshiped NIGHT and DAY,*
> *fasting and praying.*
> *Coming up to them at that very moment,*
> *she gave thanks to God and spoke about the child*
> *to all who were*
> *looking forward to the redemption of Jerusalem."*
> *Luke 2:36-38*

Anna had positioned herself for the promise! In the fullness of time, at the appointed hour the Son of God, the promise of Israel entered the temple where Anna had faithfully waited. Once again a waiting heart had found its reward.

The scriptures give us an account of others who waited, others who journeyed. The Book of Acts records the waiting of the believers in the Upper Room. These faithful followers of the risen Lord awaited His manifest presence with a steadfast heart and a spirit of unity. The Comforter was sent and once again many hundreds of lives were transformed by His arrival.

My travels pale in comparison to the journey of the Wise Men, those wanderers of old who relentlessly pursued that which gave evidence to our Lord's dwelling place. Days and hours of searching were rewarded as they gazed upon the face of their new King.

There are so many examples clearly showing us that in 'The Fullness of Time' He does come. Indeed the Prophet Joel knew this to be true. He records this promise to all believers . . .

"And afterward, I will pour out my Spirit on ALL people.
Your sons and daughters will prophesy,
your old men will dream dreams,
your young men will see visions.
Even on my servants,
both men and women,
I will pour out my Spirit in those days."
Joel 2:28-29

I encourage you to make this journey in your heart. Pursue His presence. No matter how long you have waited, I know He will come.

Let your heart remain steadfast, hoping and watching.

Be confident in the knowledge that He desires to meet you . . .

All of you . . .

In The Fullness of Time . . .

* * * *

I Love Jesus

GARBAGE CANS

45

*"O Lord, baptize our hearts into a sense
of the conditions and need of all men."*
George Fox

It is always a pleasure for me when I receive an invitation to preach somewhere. Actually, I take this responsibility very seriously. It is extremely important that I hear from the Lord what He would have me to say for that time, and for that people.

I have established a preparation routine ... most people in the churches we have pastored are familiar with it. In fact, it has become rather a joke to many!

I do most of my sermon preparation in bed! Not actually in bed of course, I sit on top of my bed with my Bibles, study books, sermon and illustration files, paper and pens all in one massive pile around me. I really don't know why or when this habit began, it was probably just the most comfortable place I could find! There I sit in the middle of this mess and endeavor to become holy.

Actually it really does become holy ground for me. I always spend precious time talking to Him. His heart pours into mine. My heart becomes a sponge, soaking in His presence.

There is one occasion however that I will always remember as I had some obvious lessons the Lord wanted to teach me. He has asked me to share them with you ...

We were pastoring close to the city of Toronto. Murray had some hospital visitation to do in the city and would be away for the whole day. The children were both in school and would also be away from home until late afternoon. This was perfect for me as I had been invited to preach a Sunday morning service in a nearby city and this was my opportunity to prepare without any distractions. Not even bothering to get dressed I surrounded myself with my books and started to prepare.

There was one problem however. It was garbage day. Before Murray left he had reminded me to listen for the sound of the truck coming so that I would remember to bring the cans into the garage once they had been emptied. Normally this job could wait for his return, however, it was an incredibly windy day and he could not bear the thought of losing those precious cans! I don't know about most men, but my husband is sure attached to those garbage cans of his. I gave him my promise, but inwardly thought his request very annoying. I was working on a sermon and had much more important things on my mind!

Once he left, I jumped back into bed, surrounded myself with my necessities and began my quiet time with God. It was just as always . . . wonderful. The rich presence of God was in the room and truths quickly began to pour out of my heart onto the paper. After several moments of basking in His presence however, I tuned in to a rather loud noise outside. Peeking out the window I was confronted with the dreaded garbage truck. I did what any normal 'spiritual' person would do under the circumstances. I ignored it. I was on 'Holy Ground' and I certainly don't do garbage when I'm on Holy Ground!

I could hear the wind howling, I knew it was very bad out there however I continued to write and to study. This went on for a very long time until finally the intensity of the wind outside drew me to the window. I was immediately faced with very bad news. There were no garbage cans in sight, which could only mean trouble for me!

Looking like anybody who has spend an entire night and most of a day in bed, I quickly ran downstairs. I had no makeup on, my hair wasn't brushed and I was still wearing my nightclothes. Most of the time I am very aware of my appearance however I had no opportunity for vanity as I needed to get to those garbage cans as quickly as I possibly could. I pulled a heavy winter coat over my nightwear, boots over my bare feet and I ran out into the wind! Off I went chasing those ridiculous garbage cans muttering all manner of unkind words for Murray. I had not only lost my sermon concentration, I had probably lost any ounce of respect the neighbors may have had for me after witnessing this wild woman chasing garbage cans down the street.

It turned out to be quite an endeavor. One garbage can was way down at the end of our street. The other one had blown completely out of sight and around the corner of yet another street. After quite some time and effort, they were eventually retrieved and our marriage restored once again.

It was while I was trudging down the road with garbage cans in both hands that I heard that very familiar voice. I really wasn't in the mood to listen. Feeling rather irritated I asked the Lord couldn't He please hold that thought till the garbage cans and I arrived safely home. I needed to get back to my 'holy ground' where surely I could hear His voice more clearly than carrying garbage cans down a windy street in my pajamas.

The tugging at my heart continued.

I listened.

I crawled back into bed that day weeping from what I knew with certainty the Lord had spoken to me on that walk home. I was very absorbed in what I was doing for the Lord. It was 'holy'. It was 'spiritual'. I was warm and cozy, safely tucked away in my hideaway with God. He was meeting me in that place and filling me with good news for His people. How could I leave such an atmosphere to retrieve some silly garbage cans! He had other plans . . .

He reminded me once again of how we as Christians can get it so mixed up. While we are safe and warm enjoying the presence of God, indeed even doing the work of God, there are lives being blown away. Lives filled with garbage, people the world and even The Church has chosen to ignore.

They don't always smell very nice. They remind us of all that is wrong in our society. However, while we stay tucked away in our comfort zones, not ready or willing to venture out, the winds of this world are blowing hard and strong taking the lost further away from our reach.

My whole sermon changed that day. I had just lived it.

We all need to listen. We need to leave the safety and comfort of our churches and spiritual experiences and run. Don't stop to consider what you may look like. Know there are precious lives being swept away by the enemy while we sleep! They may not seem important to us; however, they have a Father who loves them. He wants to remove the garbage and bring them back to the safety of His protective covering, safe from the storms that rage outside.

We as the Church of Jesus Christ have become His bride. We need to value that which is close to His heart. We need to make His heartbeat our own. He may not be physically seen among us; however, He has left us with a final request. He has asked us to listen for the cries of the lost and bring them safely home.

Sometimes the church has remained in bed. It is time to get up.

God changed my heart once again that day. Let Him change yours.

The cost is high, however, the reward is a life snatched from an eternity without God.

I still do my sermon preparation in bed . . . God still talks with me.

I do know better when it's time to get up.

* * * *

I Love Jesus

THE STRIPPER

"The dew of compassion is a tear."- - Lord Byron

Somehow I knew when she walked through the doors of our store that she was a Stripper. I also knew He had sent her to me. On the outside her countenance looked tired, tough, defensive, and very angry. However, I saw much more. One of the girls I work with informed me whom I was dealing with. I told her that somehow I already knew. I also told her to watch, as I believe my God had a special purpose for our meeting that day.

As I waited on her with what I hope was love and compassion, her story began to unfold. She was indeed tired and angry. She hated what she did for a living and as a result she hated herself. She had come into the store as the other girls she worked with had taken her clothes when she was out and had left her with nothing. She trusted no one. Her walls were huge.

My heart broke for her. I wanted to take her in my arms and hold on tight. Before I could do that however she needed to trust me and know that I truly cared. I helped her pick out some purchases and then let her into a change room to try them on. I started to walk away when I heard Him whisper that I needed to stay. I stood outside the door with my hands on the wall and began to pray and intercede for the lost lamb inside. God heard my prayer. I knew He would. This was His idea all along.

She left the change room and walked over to the cash register to pay for her purchases. It was there that her walls came tumbling down. It was a miracle really; there was no one else in the store. Just myself, my stripper, and another employee who stood in shock as she witnessed what my God was doing. The young girl very suddenly opened up. She began to pour out her heart as she told me bits and pieces of her life story. She did have a good job not too long ago, however, she had been laid off. She was left with no money and no way to provide for herself, thus, the 'new career'. With tears in her eyes she told me that she knew I had seen right through her cover. I told her I had, and most importantly, HE did. I was able to tell her what happened the moment she had entered that store. I shared with her how I had heard His voice calling me to love her that day, to love her as He did.

Her next words broke my heart. She had been planning to kill herself, as she was unable to live any longer with the guilt and torment that accompanied her lifestyle. She felt so dirty, so guilty. These feelings were magnified by the fact that she had known the Good Shepherd at one time, however, had walked away. Her personal condemnation was so great she dared not believe He would forgive her for how she was living.

What an absolute blessing as right in the middle of that store I was able to share with her the incredible grace and mercy of Jesus. I shared scriptures with her . . . words that confirmed her value and worth and His never-ending love for her. She asked me to write them down so she could go home and read them for herself. I was thrilled to oblige! We finally exchanged names, finished our conversation, and then she left. She disappeared from my life and I've never seen her since.

I do know with absolute certainty God had a purpose for our meeting that day. There were lessons to learn and lessons to share. You see, there are hundreds of millions of lost and dying people all around us. We cross paths with them every day. We may work beside them; we may even live with them. They need to know our Saviors love. He has sent you and I to tell them.

Listen to the words recorded in the Book of Matthew 9:36 . . .

> *"When he saw the crowds, he had compassion on them,*
> *because they were harassed and helpless,*
> *like sheep without a shepherd."*

Our Lord looked on the crowds with compassion. He saw their unspoken pain. He pictured them lost, alone and helpless, outside of the protective and loving care of the Shepherd.

He now asks you and I to watch carefully for these little lambs. Listen closely to the silent sounds of their pain. Take them by the hand and tenderly guide them back to the Shepherd's arms. You will find Him waiting with His arms open wide. There is absolutely no sin too great for His mercy and grace.

There is a song I sang in my teens.

You may need to sing it to someone today.

We all need to sing it to Him . . .

> *"Shepherd of Love*
> ***You knew I had gone astray.***
> *Shepherd of Love*
> *You cared that I'd lost my way.*
> *You sought and found me*
> *placed around me*
> *strong arms that carried me home.*
> *No foe can harm me*
> *nor alarm me*
> *Never again will I roam.*
> *Shepherd of Love*
> *Saviour and Lord and Guide.*
> *Shepherd of Love*
> *Forever I'll stay by your side."*
> *John W. Peterson*

Forever He will stay by you . . .

* * * *

I Love Jesus

MOVED WITH COMPASSION 47

*"What value has compassion that
does not take its object in its arms."*
- - Antoine de Saint Exupery

I can't remember her name. I don't know where she came from, or where she lived, however, I will never forget her . . .

We were pastoring in Alliston, Ontario at the time. I was still very young as were my children. Those years were so full of responsibility. As with most young mothers, I often neglected myself in order to give my time and energy to the raising of my family. I found child-rearing to be one of the most fulfilling endcavors of my entire life, at the same time, the most self-sacrificing.

I was also a Pastor's wife during those years I loved to give of myself to my congregation often nurturing and caring for them as I would my own family. Both callings led me down many different roads and took me on many different journeys. My feet were often tired, as was my entire body.

One of the women who attended our church was having company for the week. Two of her very closest friends were coming to visit and she invited me over to visit with them. There was a bonus; one was a hair-stylist who had offered to treat me to a free hair cut and style. I was thrilled! Of course I said yes, and, do take your time!

Something else happened that day, something so incredibly tender and touching I actually find it hard to put words on paper to describe the moment. I was totally relaxed and enjoying my special attention with the hairstylist when the other friend appeared. I could tell at first glance she was not only physically beautiful, but there was something else that emanated from her.

She talked with me for a while before she left us once again. Within moments she returned and asked if she could interrupt our conversation, as she needed to ask something of me. "No problem" I replied, "Ask away".

Tears filled her eyes as she explained to me what had been happening to her in those few moments she had been apart from us. She had been praying, talking with Him. He had asked her to do something for me. Something very different, yet, profoundly moving for both of us. He had asked her to wash my feet just as He had done for His disciples so very long ago.

I could not reply. My only answer was the tears that streamed down my face. She prepared a bowl of water and a cloth and knelt at my feet. I felt the cleansing power of love in her hands. Compassion flowed from every fiber of her being as she lovingly washed the feet of a perfect stranger. I experienced an incredible release as she began to minister and pray for me. The years of serving and giving to others seemed so insignificant in light of this act. I have never seen her since that day, yet she lives forever in my memory. A picture of selfless love lingers on.

You see, she followed the example of the one she called Lord. Jesus did the same thing. He washed the feet of those disciples who had faithfully journeyed beside Him. He knew they were tired. He also knew their hearts needed to learn the lessons of humility, compassion, and servant-hood. Their Master would be leaving them soon and there remained a world to reach with His message of love. Many would be coming to them with heavy hearts, their feet tired and dusty from their journeys. They would need to experience the healing hands of those who had learned at the feet of the Master.

These loyal followers of Christ would not be left alone as He had left them with the promise that He journeyed with them . . . inside their very beings. His hands would strengthen their own as they busied them-selves touching, loving and serving.

How about you . . . do you know those whose feet have become weary from the journey?

Stretch out your hands . . .

Allow compassion to motivate you to action . . .

Be His hands reaching out to a world that needs to know our Saviors love, and ultimately, His touch.

Join with me . . . put your hands in the living water and be poured out on a tired and thirsty world.

* * * *

I Love Jesus

HOLDING HANDS

48

"For I am the Lord, your God,
who takes hold of your right hand and says to you,
do not fear; I will help you."
Isaiah 41:13

My daughter is a teenager and we still hold hands! It's a wonderful feeling. There are times we'll be walking in a mall together and I will feel her slip her hand into mine. I hold on tightly, proud that the beauty by my side belongs to me . . . amazed that at her age she still wants to identify with the older woman walking by her side.

I love this verse in Isaiah. I have loved it for many years and for many reasons. In my mind I picture myself holding tightly to the hand of my Heavenly Father. I find comfort in knowing that regardless of my appearance or status in life, He still desires to walk beside me, His Hand in mine.

When Allyssa was a small child I clung to her hand for different reasons than I do today. Sometimes it was motivated by fear. I held on tightly not wanting her to get lost or hurt in any way. Her little hand in mine gave me the assurance that she was with me, under my watchful and protective care.

How like our Heavenly Father. He tells us not to be afraid. He knows that when we hold tightly to His mighty hand we remain under the umbrella of His care. There He lovingly guides us weaving our way through the maze of life and the mass of the crowd that so often can leave us lost and confused.

Just as my daughter longs to associate herself with her parent, I want to be identified with Him. You see, holding His Hand shows the world who

I belong to. Father and daughter walking side by side, hand in hand.

Hopefully, I resemble Him. I want the world to see His face reflected in mine. I desire my walk to imitate His, my conversation to be a reflection of our time spent together and our love for one another unquestionable to those watching.

My Father has asked me to share this love. In fact, He has asked me to hold out my hand offering others the opportunity to join us. In our family there is no room for exclusion. Appearance, intellect, social standing or any other factor remains unimportant to our Father. His children bear the image of their Heavenly Father and He longs to reach out His hand to all who will take hold.

The invitation has been given . . .

Hopefully, many will join us in this wonderful family where the Father and the Child walk together . . .

Hand in Hand.

* * * *

I Love Jesus

THE ANNOINTING

"The Spirit of the Sovereign Lord is on me,
because the Lord has anointed me to preach good news to the poor.
He has sent me to bind up the brokenhearted,
to proclaim freedom for the captives and release from darkness for the
prisoners,
to proclaim the year of the Lord's favor and the day of vengeance of our God,
to comfort all who mourn, and provide for those who grieve in Zion -
to bestow on them a crown of beauty instead of ashes,
the oil of gladness instead of mourning, and a garment of praise instead of
despair.
They will be called oaks of righteousness, a planting of the Lord for the display
of his splendor."
Isaiah 61:1-3

Have you ever felt the presence of the Sovereign Lord on your life?

Have you ever experienced the divine awareness of His voice calling?

As do most little girls, I delighted in play, fantasy and dress up. I took pleasure in everything that accompanied childhood and innocence. Yet, there were times that the knowledge of His presence would interrupt my play and childlike thoughts. I distinctly remember those moments in my young life. It was as though I could hear his heart calling mine.

Over the years this awareness has grown along with the desire to fulfill what God would have for all of us who are willing. A world waits to see what we will do with the instructions we have received from the heart of God . . .

I believe He asks us to preach the Good News from the platform of our own life experience. To bind up the brokenhearted with the same loving tenderness that bound our own bleeding hearts. To proclaim freedom to the captives because we were blind but now we see. To release the prisoners from darkness into light because He has turned our darkness into light and even the darkest night is not too far from His love. To proclaim the year of the Lord's favor and the day of vengeance of our God as we march through our cities and land proclaiming a mighty, strong, and, all consuming God. To comfort those who mourn because he has dried our tears . . . to offer garments of praise instead of the rags of despair and a Crown of Beauty because He bore the Crown of Thorns.

In the forest of humanity we are called to stand out tall and strong. Tree's of righteousness planted by the Lord's own hand, a display of His splendor . . .

Many times those of us, who call ourselves by His name, become confused as to the whole concept of 'preaching the good news'. Many feel unqualified, too shy, even apathy can claim a place in our hearts as we struggle with the commission that has been left to all of us. How quick we are to share a recipe, a new hit in the fashion world, a decorating tip, or even the latest hairstyle, yet find ourselves hesitant or even reticent to spread the most amazing news this world will ever hear.

Several years ago, I learned a valuable lesson that hopefully you will allow me to deposit into your heart . . .

My daughter Allyssa was just starting school full time. As I have previously confessed, I do tend to have 'overprotective' qualities! Since she had quite a long walk home, and was still only five years old, I would meet her at the school to either walk or drive her home. I decided I'd be the best overprotective mother in the neighborhood and arrive at the school early enough to meet with the other overprotective mothers, and maybe this weakness of mine could be channeled into something positive!

As it turns out, I am not alone in this dreadful disease! The schoolyard was actually quite full of others just like me! It was while I was standing somewhat impatiently waiting for Allyssa to be released, I felt that familiar tug in my heart . . .

Many times I have consecrated my life at altars, many times I have wept for the lost, yet walked away wondering when and where the opportunity would arise. While standing there, I heard His voice ever so gently remind me of all those tears I'd spent, all those calls I'd answered and knew that my mission field lay before me. It was difficult to stop the flow of tears as I gazed upon the face of woman after woman who had never heard or responded to the 'good news'.

Right away I began to pray that the Lord would lead me to those whom I was to begin a relationship with. It was an incredibly exciting time . . . friendships were made and the message was shared. There was one woman in particular who seemed to be like a sponge. The good news was definitely taking root in the soil of her heart. Her daughter Jennifer and my daughter had struck up a friendship and as time passed the bond of friendship extended to the entire family. It came to the place where I was able to invite Sandy to our church. Our ladies group had been hosting a fashion show and it seemed to be the perfect opportunity to bring her along. I'll never forget that evening . . . Sandy wandered around that church like a person just released from the desert into an oasis. Within weeks, she responded to the love of Jesus and on a Sunday night her and her two children walked to the altar, where they committed their lives to Jesus Christ forever. Within months, her husband Brian walked the same aisle and the family was complete in Him.

We need to understand that all around us there are those waiting to be released from the darkness of their night into the glorious light of His presence. I waited for my daughter in the brightness of day; however, I was surrounded by the night. The Lord placed the flame of His love into the candle of my heart and I witnessed the night become light around me.

How about you, do you long to extend the light of His love into your neighborhood, your workplace, and your life experience?

He came for those reasons. His voice continues to call you and I. His mandate remains until the final moment when He gathers His children Home.

Are you willing to hear His call?

Are you willing to say yes?

Know that you don't walk alone . . . for the Spirit of the Sovereign Lord will rest upon you!

* * * *

I Love Jesus

ABOUT THE AUTHOR

The following are a few of the conference and workshop titles that Heather has developed. There are other topics and workshops available, many of which are covered in the book.

Fruit of the Wilderness

Hosea 2:14- gives us this tender invitation . . . "Therefore I am now going to allure her; I will lead her into the desert and speak tenderly to her. There I will give her back her vineyards, and will make the Valley of Achor (Valley of Trouble) a door of hope. There she will sing as in the days of her youth, as in the day she came up out of Egypt." . . .

Many times on this journey through life, we encounter desert experiences - periods of wilderness, loneliness and seeming unfruitfulness. This scripture shows us that we have been given a divine invitation to the wilderness with the Lover of our souls. In fact His voice tenderly calls us apart to that quiet place with Him. Discover the beauty of the journey and the resources we have been given to make the desert a place of refreshing. Understand why He calls us apart and the fruit that will be developed in our life as a result of our time alone with Him.

He said Yes and Dancing in the Dark.

God has given His blessing on the ministry of women. Understand the calling Jesus Christ has placed on women and the ability he gives to be effective handmaidens in a world desperate for Him. There are however, some obstacles we encounter as we endeavour to work in His Kingdom. Dancing in the dark talks about issues that cause our feet to stumble and make us less effective in our ministry efforts. Some obstacles include jealousy, competition, identity and self-worth. God wants to release His women into effective ministry and as Habakkuk 3:19 so beautifully states . . . "The Sovereign Lord is my strength; he makes my feet like the feet of a deer, he enables me to go on the heights."

Discovering Divine Romance

St. Augustine once said "Thou hast made us for thyself, O Lord; and our hearts are restless until they rest in thee." We were created to know God and to walk in intimacy with our Lord. There is a divine romance that waits for all of us. Understand that from the very beginning we were created for communion with God. In His divine plan He made provision for us to be reconciled with Him through the laying down of His Son. There are however, obstacles that keep us from knowing God in all His fullness. We examine the lives of some amazing women from the Bible and learn through their experiences how to overcome the obstacles to discovering divine romance.

Journey through the Seasons of a Woman

For some change is exciting and refreshing. For others, change brings pain and insecurity. A women's life is a constantly changing experience. Some changes are welcome and invited; others seem to be an interruption and inconvenience. We look at the changes and developments in a woman's life from the dreams and desires of a young girl and discover the beauty and excitement that God has planned for every season in our life.

All Broken Up and Nowhere to Go!

Have you ever looked at others and wondered why their world seems so perfect and yours so not!

Understand that God has placed incredible value in our brokenness. In fact He values that which often others do not. Take your broken and cracked places and allow the light of God's presence to shine through you making you a vessel that brings change and impact to those around you.

Heather may be reached at...

heather@lifeconceptministries.com
www.lifeconceptministries.com